SHARMA KRAUSKOPF is a writer and speaker on 'All Things Scottish' and lighthouses. Her husband, Dean Krauskopf, is an agricultural advisor employed by Michigan State University. Dean hosts the popular 'Gardening Show' broadcast on WJR radio in Detroit. A farm in Parma, Michigan is home most of the year. Their home from home, where they live for the rest of the year, is Eshaness Lighthouse in the Shetland Islands.

For twenty years Sharma was an administrator and consultant to social service programs serving the poor and/or disadvantaged. She is now editor, writer, and webmaster for www.scottishradiance.com, a successful internet magazine with over 1.5 million visitors a month. Scottish Radiance is one of the most highly regarded sites on the web for quality of presentation and content, with regular contributions from well-known Scottish writers. Awards include USA Today Hot Spot, US Scots Five Stars, Celtic Site of the year, and many more.

Equally at home writing adult and children's books, two of her most recent books are Scotland – A Complete Guide and Road Atlas (Appletree Press, 2000; published in the US by Globe Pequot Press as Scotland: The Complete Guide) and Moonbeam Cow (Richard B. Owens, 2000), a children's book on how the Belted Galloway got its name.

Sharma features on the recent video Scottish Lighthouses (produced by Morgan Video Productions, 6312 SW Capitol Highway #245, Portland, Oregon 97201) and also on a forthcoming BBC documentary on lighthouse living. The lighthouse itself features in the song 'Eshaness' specially written by Moira Kerr for her CD Time and Tide (CDMAYK14, released by Mayker Records Limited, PO Box 887, Glasgow G52 1EL).

The Last Lighthouse

SHARMA KRAUSKOPF

Luath Press Limited

EDINBURGH

www.luath.co.uk

First edition 2000

An edited version of 'Why Lighthouses?' (pp 59-62) was first published in the February 2000 issue of *Lighthouse Digest* (PO Box 1690, Wells, Maine 04090, USA; tel: 001 207 646 0515; e: lhdigest@lhdigest.com).

The paper used in this book acid-free, neutral-sized and recyclable. It is made from low chlorine pulps produced in a low energy, low emission manner from sustainable forests.

Printed and bound by
Bell & Bain Ltd., Glasgow

Typeset in 10.5 point Sabon by
S. Fairgrieve and A. Drews, Edinburgh

Map by Jim Lewis

This book is dedicated to my dear friend 'Susie' (Sue Frye), whose support made this story possible, and to the caretaker at Eshaness, Tom Williamson, who has become my teacher in 'all things Shetland' and an adopted member of our family.

A NOTE ON SPELLING

Most of the spelling and terminology in this book is US English. You will however find signs of my picking up some UK English, and Scots.

0 10 20 30 40 50 60 70 80 Kilometres

0   10   20   30   40   50 Miles

Eshaness

Lerwick

Cape Wrath   *Strathy Point*   *Duncansby Head*

Butt of Lewis   Thurso   *Noss Head*

Neist Point   Portree

Inverness

SCOTLAND

Oban

Rinns of Islay

Glasgow   Edinburgh

Mull of Kintyre   *Turnberry*
Ailsa Craig

Corsewall   Stranraer

NORTHERN
IRELAND

ENGLAND

6

Contents

7

8

Introduction

Dreams do come true. Everyone at some time or other fantasizes about what would make his or her life perfect. Usually it is just a momentary thought and then we go about our daily lives. For an agricultural advisor and a writer/webmaster living on farm in Midwestern United States to live at a remote Scottish lighthouse keeper's home seemed only a flight of the imagination. The more we thought about a lighthouse home the more we wanted it. Following the philosophy if 'you don't shoot any arrows you won't hit anything' we decided to try to buy a Scottish lighthouse home. Walt Whitman's words in 'The Leaves of Grass' helped us sail forth on our adventure.

The untold want, by life and land ne'er granted,
Now, Voyager, sail thou forth, to seek and find.

It took eight years to make our dream come. Important terms in that last sentence are 'make the dream'. Our success did not come about without a lot of hard work, sacrifice, patience and resiliency. We learned you do not just dream and wait for something to happen. You grab hold of that hope, hold on with everything in you and focus all of your energy to make it come to pass.

The following is not a story of my husband and I running away from the chaos and the stress of American life. Our intent was always to become a part of something extraordinary. We were not running away from the United States but toward Scotland, a beautiful county, and its culture. At the end of our adventure we found great peace and serenity in our beautiful lighthouse home, but that was not our main objective.

The story started with a traditional Scottish 'sheep jam' on the Isle of Skye. While trapped by those sheep my love affair with Scotland began. I longed to become a part of Scotland somehow. A few weeks ago I saw a logo that communicates perfectly how I feel about Scotland. It said, 'American First, Scottish Always'. To be fair, my husband wasn't quite as wrapped up in 'the Scotland Thing', as our grown children call it, as I was, but it didn't take long before he was as caught up in it too.

This book relates the various stages Dean and I went through to secure our lighthouse, including how we are learning to live in the Shetland Islands now. There are many who may think going to live at a remote lighthouse as far north as the Shetland Islands is more like suffering from insanity than going to paradise. For us remoteness and a lighthouse was always what we wanted. How it came to be in the Shetland Islands was a stroke of luck.

The story is mainly told through a series of e-mails written as the events unfolded. Some of the e-mails contained in the section entitled 'The Search' were created from other sources such as hard copy correspondence or faxes. For those of you not familiar with e-mail, the heading for each letter has the date, the subject of the e-mail and to whom it is being sent. Most of the e-mails are addressed to 'Susie', which is a pet name for Sue Frye, my dearest friend for over twenty-five years. We have been through a lot together, including Sue's fight with and victory over cancer. It was only natural for me to turn to her for support as all this transpired. As it turned out she was directly involved in the process as she made three trips to Scotland to help us search for the lighthouse. She was with us when we finally found 'the perfect one'. Once in a while you will come across an e-mail addressed to 'rampaint', which means it was sent to my brother. I sent some to myself just to keep track of events which are addressed to sjk@world.net. A great many of the e-mails from Eshaness are addressed to @LIST5E23.PML, which is a group of friends to whom my computer's software sends an individually addressed e-mail. When I started LIST5E23 there were only a few names on the list but the recipients enjoyed it so much they told their friends and the list is now quite large. It was the members of the e-mail list that convinced me to write this book. All the e-mail addresses in the book are fictitious so do not try to use them to reach anyone. You can reach me at sharma@eshanesslighthouse.co.uk.

The first section, 'The Search', details the pursuit and purchase of our Scottish lighthouse home. Scotland is 274 miles long from north to south and varies in breadth between 24 and 154 miles, and we must have covered most of its 31,510 square miles in the course of our search. Scotland had a population of 5,137,000 in 1995 with most of the people in two large cities, Edinburgh and Glasgow. The majority of our story takes place in the Highlands and Islands, where most of the country's lighthouses are located.

Scotland is a country with a long history. People associate Scotland with kilts, bagpipes, Rob Roy, Robert the Bruce, and William Wallace. This book focuses on a modern country and the beautiful lighthouses that protect the ships from the treacherous ocean surrounding it. There are few parts of the world that possess more magic and mystery than the seas around Scotland. Some six thousand miles of coastline (69% of that of the entire United Kingdom) create a wonderland of over eight hundred islands, mountains, rocks and stacks. A country of breathtaking beauty, its charm is formed not only by the proximity of its mountains to the sea, but also its geographic and geological complexity, and its unpredictable climate. It is a serene, sometimes chaotic, landscape where every region has a distinct personality. A place with differences so remarkable that merely going a few miles can be like visiting another continent, with no better example of that than the Shetland Islands.

A key element in our search was the Northern Lighthouse Board. In 1786 Parliament created the Northern Lighthouse Board, authorizing the construction of four lighthouses in Scotland (Kinnaird Head, North Ronaldsay, Scalpay and Mull of Kintyre) plus the establishment of a Commission for their operation. The original Commissioners were the law agents of the Crown, Sheriffs of coastal counties, and the Lord Provosts and Provosts of Scottish cities and towns whose mercantile interests were involved. The Board has been reorganized many times as the local political structures have changed.

The Board's principal interest is the safety of the ships and people on the sea around Scotland. The Northern Lighthouse Board manages all Scottish and the Isle of Man lighthouses, buoys and beacons. Operating costs are met from a 'General Lighthouse Fund', financed by the collection of Light Dues paid by commercial ships calling at Scottish and Isle of Man ports, and by fishing vessels over ten meters in length.

Currently the Northern Lighthouse Board manages 84 Major Automatic Lighthouses, 116 Minor Lights, 117 Buoys, 43 Unlit Beacons, 23 Racon Stations, 19 Fog Stations, and 3 DGPS (Differential Global Positioning System) Stations. They presently operate two ships, *Pharos* and *Fingal*, which deliver supplies, tend buoys, and inspect the navigation aids on oilrigs in the Scottish sector. A new ship, *Pole Star*, is to replace *Fingal* in fall of 2000.

Central to the first part of the story is the Northern Lighthouse Board's system of selling the lighthouse property and keeper's accommodations. After each automation was completed and the keepers gone, the Board sealed off the operational section of the tower from the keeper's accommodations and then sold all of the property except the still operating tower. This meant the property would be maintained but not at Northern Lighthouse Board expense. The owner of the keeper's accommodations and property around the tower must maintain it to Northern Lighthouse Board standards. So when I mention we are considering buying a certain lighthouse, it means the accommodations and land but not the tower. As long as the towers function they will belong to the Northern Lighthouse Board. A special thank you goes to the Northern Lighthouse Board staff for all their help during the course of our search.

'The Search' section e-mails cover a period of eight years beginning with the sheep jam on Skye and ending with the purchase of Eshaness Lighthouse. Between those two events we made more trips to Scotland than I can remember. Buying real estate in Scotland is different from what we were used to in the US. We got to know the Scottish system well before we were finished. Six unsuccessful bids for lighthouse accommodations were submitted during our search including two for Corsewall Point Lighthouse, one for Noss Head Lighthouse, one for Strathy Point Lighthouse, and two for Eshaness Lighthouse in the Shetland Islands.

To make it easier to follow our nightmare marathon of bid submitting, the following is a summary of the properties and submissions.

First, Corsewall Point Lighthouse located near Stranraer on the south-western coast of Scotland, looking out on Ailsa Craig and Ireland. The lighthouse was built in 1817 and designed by Robert Stevenson. The facility was automated in 1994. We made two unsuccessful bids, one in 1994 and one in 1995, to the Northern Lighthouse Board for the three keeper's accommodations, bothy, and garage plus land.

Second, Noss Head Lighthouse located on the far north-eastern coast of the Scottish mainland, a couple of miles north of Wick. The station was built in 1849 and designed by Alan Stevenson. We made one unsuccessful bid to a private owner for three keeper's accommodations, a stone steading, and twenty acres in 1997.

Third, Strathy Point Lighthouse located on the northern coast of the Scottish mainland, between Bettyhill and Thurso. This station was built in 1958, making it the last manned lighthouse built by the Northern Lighthouse Board. The designer was Peter H. Hyslop. The facility was automated in 1997 and we made one unsuccessful bid to the Northern Lighthouse Board in 1998 for three keeper's accommodations and three garages.

Fourth, Eshaness Lighthouse located on the north-western coast of the main island in the Shetland Island group. Eshaness was built in 1929 and designed by David A. Stevenson. It was the last lighthouse designed by a member of the world famous Stevenson family of lighthouse engineers. The station was automated in 1974. We made two unsuccessful bids to a private owner in 1999 for one-keeper accommodation, a storage facility and a garage.

Thousands of dollars were spent on solicitors, faxes, telephone calls, and postage during the bid process. We spent many sleepless nights and shed some tears. There are some large breaks of time between e-mails in 'The Search' section narrative. I have tried to indicate the elapsed period in the body of the e-mails but you can also look at the dates.

With our third bid we succeeded in buying Eshaness Lighthouse keeper's accommodations and property in the Shetland Islands. In the last part of this book Eshaness Lighthouse and Shetland Islands are the center of the activity. The Shetland Islands are a group or chain of many islands called an archipelago. The group consists of around one hundred islands, some 550 square miles in area with 3,000 miles of coastline and a population of approximately 23,000. Most people on the UK mainland and beyond think of the Shetland Isles as a peripheral region somewhere up at the top of the map of Great Britain. The Shetlands are often omitted altogether from UK maps. Shetland is near the North Atlantic's fertile fishing grounds and major oil reserves and as close to Norway as it is to Aberdeen. Revenue from the extraction of offshore oil from the 1970s onwards has supplemented income from the traditional sheep, cattle, and knitwear industries. The largest oil terminal in Europe is located in the Shetlands at Sullom Voe.

Eshaness Lighthouse is located on the north-western coast of the largest island often called 'Mainland' by Shetlanders. To find Eshaness on a Shetland map look north of Mavis Grind, a 100-yard strip of land separating the Atlantic Ocean from the North Sea. Mavis Grind means gate of the narrow isthmus and the Grind does nearly cut the island in half. Eshaness is located in the region called Northmavine. The area is composed mainly of red granite and diorite, a place both wild and glorious, with some of the best scenery in Shetland.

The nearest village to Eshaness Lighthouse is Hillswick. Hillswick is well known as the home of the St Magnus Hotel, a wooden building prefabricated in Norway to be used at the Great Exhibition in Glasgow in 1896. Purchased by the North of Scotland Orkney and Shetland Steam Navigation Company, the St Magnus was re-built at Hillswick in 1902.

The road to the lighthouse turns west off of the Hillswick road. The Eshaness peninsula has a unique remote and rugged beauty. Many feel that it has some of the most beautiful seascapes in the world with numerous sea stacks and natural arches. There is much to do, including wandering for hours along the cliffs, watching the birds, searching the beaches for shells and driftwood or exploring the fishing stations of the past at Stenness beach.

The 'Getting Ready' section tells of the joy and the excitement preparing for the first trip to our new lighthouse home at Eshaness. Because we had to pay more for the property than we originally planned the biggest challenge was to furnish our new home with almost no money. That is easier to do if you can use second-hand furniture and garage sale items, but I was four thousand miles away from Eshaness when we purchased it. I looked into shipping used furniture and the cost was prohibitive.

We became the owners of Eshaness keeper's accommodations on 1 May 1999 so the next group of letters was written during the trip to take possession of the property. The excitement, and trepidation, was heightened when I learned that Dean could not come with me on this trip. I was more than a little apprehensive about going alone to a remote place where I had spent a sum-total of about 72 hours. Another fear for both of us was whether, after going through so much to get our lighthouse property, it would live up to our expectations. There was no way I could have anticipated how much I would come to love our little home on the ocean's edge and how much joy and beauty it would give me even without furniture. Because of our lack of funds I had only a table, bed, futon chair and a TV to make me comfortable on that first trip. Thank goodness the house had a new stove, refrigerator, freezer and a bright red shiny Rayburn. The days I spent there that May were some of the happiest in my life.

Tom Williamson's name appears throughout the Eshaness e-mails. He is the wonderful person who became the caretaker of our lighthouse. He has lived on the island most of his life except for the years he spent in the merchant marine. Now he is a crofter along with his full time job as the night watchman for a salmon fish hatchery. Tom became my 'living in Shetland tutor'. Without him adapting to Eshaness would have been a lot more difficult. I have come to love and respect Tom deeply.

The May trip was so incredible that coming back to the US was difficult. The 'Back in the USA' section tells how Dean and I planned another trip in September. During this period I struggled to buy more furnishings for our new home with our limited resources. We wanted Sue and my brother and sister-in-law to visit in September. More furniture was needed as we couldn't ask them all to sleep on the floor in one room. Everything that could go wrong during that period of time did.

The final section 'Scotland in September' is the journal of my second trip. This includes Dean's first opportunity to spend a significant period of time at his new home.

I am now back on Shetland again as I write this. The story has not ended and I will continue to send my e-mails to my list. Who knows there may be enough great adventures to bring about a second book about life at Eshaness?

Sharma Krauskopf
Eshaness, September 2000

PART ONE

The Search

Date sent: Tuesday, 24 September 1991
Subject: **Bewitched by Scotland**
To: Susie@world.net

Susie,

Having heard a lot about spells and second sight during my six or seven previous visits to Scotland, I never thought I would have premonitions. Dean, brother Ray, sister-in-law Marylou and I were on our way to stay at Orbost Farm, a bed and breakfast south of Dunvegan on the Isle of Skye yesterday. Driving along a single-track road leading to the B&B we saw a mass of white coming down the hill in front of us; as we got nearer we could tell it was a large flock of sheep, driven by two men and five dogs. Within minutes our road was barricaded by hundreds of sheep. Caught in a Hebridean Island 'sheep jam' we could either turn around on the narrow road or wait until the sheep choose to let the cars use the road again. Turning around was dangerous and at the end of the road was our bed for the night so, being in no particular hurry, we decided to wait. If you have to be trapped by a flock of sheep there is no more beautiful place for it to happen. On our right were MacLeod's Tables with their flat tops touching the sky and on our left green hills containing many tiny white croft houses sparkling in the sun. In front of us beyond the long creeping line of sheep was the sparkling, dark green water of the sea. The only sounds were the dogs barking and sheep bleating. We sat in this magnificent spot for fifteen minutes or more.

Fifteen minutes may seem like a long time if you are in a hurry to go somewhere; but it is a brief period for the weaving of a magical spell that could change your life forever. During the time we were stuck behind that mass of sheep, Scotland became a part of me. A spell so strong that I knew without a doubt, no matter what the future holds, I am going to find a way for this wonderful country to be in my life.

Bewitched

Date sent: Wednesday, 9 October 1991
Subject: **Genetic Problem**
To: Susie@world.net

Sue,

Back home in the United States and my desire to somehow be a
part of Scotland is as intense as it was when we got caught in the
sheep jam. Dean says it is just my Morrison genes acting up.
I was on Skye when it happened. There is some evidence
pointing to the genes since the Morrison Clan started as
solicitors to the Macleods of Skye before they moved to Lewis to
become judges. Modern science does not know all the whys and
wherefores of what genes do. Maybe my genes contain a link,
which dictate I must return home to Scotland. I am just kidding
but it is strange how Scotland has become so important. Having
traveled all over the world, no other country has had that effect.

Whatever it is, I am even more convinced that Scotland fits
into my future.

Sharma 'Morrison' Krauskopf

Date sent: Wednesday, 18 November 1991
Subject: **Twins**
To: Susie@world.net

Sue,

Don't panic – I am not pregnant nor are either of my daughters.
I have linked Hilltop Farm Bed & Breakfast to Orbost Bed &
Breakfast. Orbost owned by the Macdonald family is the B&B we
were on our way to visit them when we got caught in the sheep
jam in September. It was Orbost Farm sheep that caused the
'problem'. We do not hold that against the Macdonalds but kid
them a lot about it.

This linking process is what the Scots call 'twinning'. It
means we promote each other's establishment with brochures

and refer people back and forth. I have decorated one of our rooms with pictures of Skye and named it the 'Isle of Skye' room. Margaret Macdonald has been sharing recipes with me so I now serve a Scottish high tea to our guests. I bake an excellent scone these days.

This has lead to more contact between the Macdonalds, the owners of Orbost Farm Bed & Breakfast and us. This seemed like a good first step in getting more involved with Scotland. We are scheduling a trip to visit Orbost Farm next year. I think I should test out whether or not this 'Scotland Thing' is just some fantasy or real enough that I would be happy to spend extended periods of time in Scotland.

Operator of the US Twin Bed and Breakfast

Date sent: Tuesday, 28 January 1992
Subject: **Macdonalds**
To: Susie@world.net

Hi!

We're just back from another trip to Scotland to further test whether our feelings toward Scotland are the same. We spent two weeks with the Macdonalds at Orbost Farm. They are becoming a big part of keeping Scotland in our lives. Margaret Macdonald and I seemed to be a perfect match with many of the same interests beyond our B&Bs. Robert and Dean are so much alike it is scary. How two people born on different sides of the Atlantic Ocean can be so similar is beyond me. Robert reads two newspapers a day from cover to cover just like Dean. Poor Margaret and I find ourselves talking to a newspaper not a person. If they get started talking about cattle, Margaret and I might as well watch the 'tellie' because there will no more non-bovine discussion for the rest of the evening.

We spent countless hours discussing our different cultures beside a coal fire as the wind howls outside. In fact, not once did we go to bed before two in the morning. The Macdonalds are teaching us about the real Scotland, not the idealized image of the tourist brochures but the genuine drama of people struggling in one of the most beautiful but sometimes savage places in the world. I am coming to love and respect the people of Scotland through the Macdonalds and their friends on Skye. They are definitely increasing my desire to be a part of this fantastic country. When people ask 'Why Scotland?' it is easy to say because of our friends the Macdonalds. After all, it was the Macdonalds' crazy sheep which were first responsible for my being bewitched by Scotland.

The Newspaper Widow

Date sent: Monday, 12 April 1993
Subject: **Child of the Hills**
To: Susie@world.net

Susie,

It hardly seems possible I am back in Scotland at Orbost Farm. It has been almost a year since I was here last. This morning I woke just after sunrise saw it was sunny and the air clear. The hills were sparkling jade green and the ocean a deep sapphire. As I stood at the window I noticed Sarah, the older of the Macdonald children, striding toward the gate that keeps the sheep out of the fenced garden or, as we would say in the States, the front yard. Without a fence there would be no grass or flowers anywhere in Scotland, since Scottish sheep are not the least bit fussy about what they eat. Sarah in a bright pink parka was painstakingly trying to keep mud off of her bright green boots, known here as 'wellies'. I know what you are thinking. Wellies are for puddles – but not Sarah's. Sarah's have a frog's face with yellow eyes on them and are her pride and joy. As she walked out to the stone steading (barn) I though how wonderful it was that a small child could wander so freely. People here don't lock their doors and they leave their babies in their prams outside stores. I have heard people accuse the rural and island people of Scotland of being eighty years behind the rest of the world. Well, if they are it is not a bad way to be and it just reinforces my desire to live here at least part time. I suppose eventually with all the new technology Scotland will become more like the large industrialized countries but I hope it doesn't happen in my lifetime. Dean and I have decided we will buy a retirement home in Scotland where we will spend six months, with the other six months being spent in the States on the farm.

I have started to write a story about Sarah's trip to the steading in her wonderful 'wellies' and have named it 'Child of the Hills'. I have decided another way I might become involved with this country is to write articles. Hopefully I have enough talent to make them something people will want to read.

Hopeful Writer

Date sent: Monday, 12 April 1993
Subject: **American Forever**
To: Susie@world.net

Susie,

Second letter of the day but I just had to share this. Orbost is in the middle of the lambing season. With over 1,000 sheep it as a hectic time and everyone has a job. Sarah and I bottle-feed the orphaned lambs. This afternoon Robert brought a cute newborn lamb in from the hills. Sarah and I give every one of our charges a name so we were discussing a name for this one when I suggested to Sarah we call this newcomer Sharma. Sarah looked at me with the strangest expression and said. 'No, we can't. If we called it Sharma it might talk funny like you'. So the lamb is called Moira. Once again I was gently reminded I am an American and always will be. The more time I spend here the surer I am that I want to embrace their culture and live like a

Scot. The Scots resent 'outlanders' coming and trying to impose their way of life on Scotland. I can understand why. Don't let me ever forget that I have chosen Scotland for what it is not what I think it should be.

I am here to learn not to change this wonderful country.

The Person with the Wrong Accent

Date sent: Tuesday, 13 April 1993
Subject: **The Pram that Got Away**
To: Susie@world.net

Sue,

What a horrible day this was. Margaret and I took the girls into Portree to get souvenirs for people at home. Having to get some groceries, Margaret set off for the Co-op and I took six month old Jenny and her pram to the car. Oh, I forgot to mention it was a nasty day with gale force winds. It was hard going pushing Jenny and the pram up the steep hills of Portree against the winds. Exhausted I reached the car. I parked the pram behind the car while I put Jenny in her car seat. After Jenny was safely in the car I went to back to put the pram in the boot, known in America as the 'trunk'. Guess what, the pram wasn't there. It was racing down the hill driven by the wind toward the sea. I took off running after it at high-speed. Just as I was sure the pram was about to become a boat, a large man stepped out and stopped it. I thanked him as best I could after running a couple of blocks in total panic. He just laughed when he heard my accent and said, 'If you stay on Skye long enough you will learn that the weather is always in control'. He was right. What if the pram had still had Jenny in it? The thought of it makes me nauseous. I still have a lot to learn about Scotland.

The Stupid American

Date sent: Friday, 21 January 1994
Subject: **Trip to Neist Point**
To: Susie@world.net

Hi!

Another year and we have returned to Scotland to begin our search for our Scottish retirement home.

Neist Point Lighthouse keepers' accommodation in the north-west corner of the Isle of Skye is on the market according to an advertisement I saw in *Scottish Field* magazine. The lighthouse lies near the boundary of Orbost Farm's six thousand acres so the Macdonalds would be our neighbors if you can call some one who is a couple of miles away a neighbor. Having never visited the lighthouse we decided to take a look before we seriously considered it. Two days ago, Dean, Margaret and I drove out to see Neist Point. The weather forecast was for rain and gales but Scotland's weather being so unpredictable we decided to give it a try anyway. When we reached the lighthouse's car-park heavy rain and ferocious wind had arrived before us. Getting out of the car we could barely stand against the wind. We could see a waterfall that Margaret said usually fell gently over the cliff into the sea, but not today. The winds were so strong the water would fall partially down the cliff and then be blown skyward like a geyser. This convinced us another day might be better to walk to the lighthouse.

Yesterday the sun was shining and the wind had dropped so we finally visited Neist Point Lighthouse. Dean, Margaret, Sarah, Jenny and I walked for forty-five minutes down the cliff and across the headland to reach the lighthouse. There is no car access. Neist Point is a spectacular place with panoramic views in all directions. The lighthouse is completely isolated except for an occasional tourist devoted enough to lighthouses to make the long walk out and, of course, the always-present sheep. Returning to Orbost I called the owner to make an appointment to see the inside of the buildings.

Today we visited and had tea with Neist Point's owners. Our short visit convinced Dean and I that lighthouse living would fit us perfectly. The lighthouse is so much a part of the ocean and there is a feel of history about the place. Dean loved the idea of throwing a lobster trap over the cliff and catching a fresh one for dinner. He was also delighted with the picture of the loch behind the lighthouse filled with fish. The thing that impressed me the most was that you could watch seals from the kitchen window while you did dishes.

Neist Point is like all of the Scottish lighthouse stations; you only purchase the keepers' accommodations and the land. The lighthouse towers are still operating and managed by the Northern Lighthouse Board. You have the joy of living at an operating lighthouse without responsibility for the beacon and tower.

A slight complication is that Neist Point has another potential buyer. We will just have to go home and wait until we hear from the owner. Knowing how impatient I am, that will be difficult.

Potential Lighthouse Buyer

Date sent: Tuesday, 22 February 1994
Subject: **Disappointment**
To: Susie@world.net

Sue,

Well, the wait is over. We hoped the party interested in buying Neist Point would not complete their purchase but after a month of waiting we received a fax announcing that he had in fact bought it. I was devastated and shed tears at the news. The frustrating part was we were not even allowed to submit a bid. I am more and more uneasy with the Scottish system of buying property. It frightens me because I don't understand it. In all probability we couldn't have outbid the other buyer but I would have liked to try. It made me question if all of this is just a silly fantasy and not practical. Neist Point proved that a historic lighthouse in an isolated location so close to the sea was a perfect place for us to retire.

Because of the urging of some friends who want us to stay in the States, I have done some checking in the USA and found that the prices for lighthouse property are well above what we can pay. We will continue to focus on Scotland, which was the original goal anyway. United States lighthouse prices make a Scottish lighthouse seem like a bargain. I hope I have the courage and the patience to put up with the difficulties of buying in another country using a totally different acquisition system.

Disappointed but Undaunted

Date sent: Thursday, 3 March 1994
Subject: **Recovery and Planning**
To: Susie@world.net

Susie,

After losing Neist Point, Dean and I spent hours determining what it would truly take for us to buy a lighthouse in Scotland. First thing we need is the assistance of a Scottish bank. It is too risky for the seller to negotiate with someone so far away without some kind of local security. Getting bank sponsorship should not be a big problem since we have good credit rating and references. Our biggest obstacle will be the down payment. The exchange rate varies but it could take up to 1.75 US dollars for every British Pound Sterling. We will have to find a way to secure at least $50,000 for a down payment.

Dean has a stable income that will help support the lighthouse after we buy it but we need some way to rapidly increase cash on hand. After two seconds of consideration bank robbery and extortion were ruled out, we are just not the type. We decided I would double my consulting workload to put money into what we are now calling the 'lighthouse fund'.

This means I will be traveling extensively all over the United States doing workshops with few days spent at home. To keep my spirits up as well as remind me of why I am spending so much time away from home, I will carry a picture of a Scottish Lighthouse everywhere I go. Every night as I go to sleep in hotel after hotel I will look at that picture. I read somewhere if you picture what you want long and hard your mind will find a way to get it. I will use any technique that might help.

Dean and I are making some other adjustments. Neither of us will get a new car. I will buy only the clothes I need for work. Cutting down on eating out and expensive entertainment will be necessary. Working together towards something that matters so much to both of us makes none of these sacrifices seem major. At least for now it is fun working together.

In lieu of money your donation to the fund will be to help me keep focused when I start grumbling about not being able to do or buy something which is bound to happen

On a Budget Sharma

Date sent: Wednesday, 4 May 1994
Subject: **Blessing**
To: Susie@world.net

Sue,

An unexpected blessing in our lighthouse search has been the support of hundreds of my students all over the United States. Goal setting and resiliency are part of the curriculum I teach so I am using the search for a lighthouse home as an example in the workshops. The participants are captivated by what we are trying to do. A Wyoming group sold cookies and crafts to raise money for their passports and eventual travel to visit the light-house in Scotland; in Utah the participants surprised me by decorating our training room with pictures of lighthouses; and in Washington my students gave me a lighthouse book. Without the wonderful support of these people I might give up. It is hard since I return home only to do laundry before leaving again. My health and tolerance of airplanes, hotels, and restaurants is stretched to the limit. I may have to cut back on the travel schedule if it doesn't get better.

I have started writing for a Scottish Internet Magazine located in the Highlands. I am not being paid for my writing but am learning more and more about Scotland. Maybe there is a way to turn my writing into more income so I can give up the traveling.

The guys at the Internet Magazine are not supportive of the lighthouse purchase and keep trying to convince me another type of property would be more appropriate. A surprise to me was how some people plead with us to stay closer to town and the centers of activities. The usual comment is 'It might be fine for you but I would never do it especially for retirement'. What I cannot understand is why they are so uncomfortable with what we are trying to do.

Sharma

Date sent: Thursday, 2 June 1994
Subject: **Visit to Corsewall**
To: Susie@world.net

Sue,

I am back in Scotland again. A week ago a fax came from the Northern Lighthouse Board announcing Corsewall Point Lighthouse keeper's accommodation in the Galloway area of south-western Scotland would be coming on the market in the next few weeks. I was ecstatic. Our second opportunity to purchase a Scottish lighthouse might be about to occur. Since Dean and I had never been in the south-west corner of Scotland we decided I should fly over and take a look. The area is easily reached from Glasgow by train and the train ride through the

Galloway hills was magnificent. Corsewall Point is one of the more spectacular Scottish lighthouses, sitting at sea level with the ocean in front and Loch Ryan on the right. You can see Ailsa Craig and Ireland on a good day. Engineered by Robert Stevenson in 1817 it is one of the few lighthouses with battlements, which gives it an elegant feel. The property being sold includes three keepers' houses plus a bothy. The only way we could afford to purchase it is by renting the keepers' houses out on a weekly basis, known in Scotland as self-catering. This means we will need a business loan.

I approached three Stranraer banks to see if they would help finance the purchase of Corsewall Point as a self-catering business. Convincing skeptical bankers of the profitability of operating a business at a lighthouse is not an easy task even though it is successful in other areas. Corsewall is not even in a remote location, being only ten miles from Stranraer. Two banks said 'no' immediately. Only Tom Mitchell, the business manager for Clydesdale Bank, was receptive to the idea. He instructed me to develop a business plan that would demonstrate the financial feasibility of the project.

In preparation for making a bid I have met with a solicitor, better known in the States as a lawyer. I didn't want to pay legal fees but it is obvious we cannot buy property in Scotland without a good solicitor. At least I like the solicitor and think she will stay on top of things. When you are trying to do things by long distance that is all-important.

As soon as I get home I will have to develop the business plan, which I am NOT looking forward to since it is all figures and lots of research.

The Entrepreneur

Date sent: Friday, 16 September 1994
Subject: **Business Plan for Corsewall and First Bid**
To: Susie@world.net

Ms Frye,

Developing the business plan was a struggle; since I had never done one before, to tell you the truth I hated the bloody thing. Dean is constantly reminding me I have trouble adding even with a calculator. Five-year projections are a nightmare. Tom Mitchell patiently guided me through every step and an amazing thing happened. Clydesdale Bank approved the business plan. Now we must wait for the Northern Lighthouse Board to call for public bids.

As I understand it, the purchasing process in Scotland operates in two ways. If the seller is willing, a buyer's solicitor can submit a bid at any time. If the seller feels he has more than one person interested they announce a closing date for a public bid and all interested parties' solicitors submit sealed bids. The Northern Lighthouse Board, being a body controlled by elected officials usually requires a public bid.

In Scotland you hire a surveyor/evaluator to determine the value of a property. They inspect the property and give you a detailed evaluation that sets the base price. Our survey for Corsewall Point came in well below the Northern Lighthouse Board's asking price. We have instructed our solicitors to submit a bid a little below the survey price. Buying property is always frightening but making this bid was terrifying since we were purchasing in another country, using every cent we have in the world, and would be going deeply in debt. The result was good news and bad news. We were the only bidders but the bid was too low and not accepted

Our options are to have our solicitor submit a higher bid immediately or wait and see if the Board would consider a lower price later. Right now no one else is interested. We don't know what to do. Normally you would submit a higher bid right away but, since it is late fall, we feel a bid later would be the best tactic since over the winter there should not be much new interest. Also if we submit a bid now and it was accepted we would have to support the property without any income since winter is the slowest season for self-catering. Waiting would also allow Dean, who has not seen the property except in photographs, to actually visit Corsewall Point. We will submit our next bid in January after our annual winter visit. I hope we did the right thing.

How would you like to go with us in January and see Corsewall and the Galloway area?

Hopeful,

Sharma

Date sent: Monday, 30 January 1995
Subject: **Second Visit to Corsewall and the Big Mistake**
To: Susie@world.net

Sue,

I hope you enjoyed your trip to Scotland even though you caught a terrible cold. I still can't get over how Stranraer totally shut down for four days to celebrate Hogmanay. No one warned us that New Year was a bigger holiday in Scotland than Christmas. It was wonderful the way our kind B&B hosts spent New Year's Eve with us beside the coal fire before they went 'first footing'. An even bigger gift was the wonderful dinner they left for us on New Year's Day since everything in town was closed. Dean still feels bad he did not watch the fire more closely to prevent a coal falling out and burning a small hole in the rug. It did not seem to bother them but it upset him.

New Year's Day at the Corsewall Point was glorious. Corsewall Point's attendant, Tom Kelly, was awfully nice to let us in on New Year's Day to measure the rooms. Safeway's shepherd's pie might not have been the most elegant New Year's lunch but we certainly shared it in a great place. I am glad you and Dean loved the lighthouse as much as I did. I was worried that I might have made a mistake when we made the first bid based on my evaluation alone. Remember that night having dinner with Corsewall Point's attendant at the hotel in Kirkcolm followed by the trip to see the lighthouse up close at night? By the time we arrived at the lighthouse a light snow was falling. Glancing skyward toward the tower we saw five shining shafts of light containing glittering particles of white rotating above us. Resembling the blades of the departing helicopter, the light extended out from the tower in long silver beams containing glittering snow trapped in absolute silence. What a wondrous sight in the starless sky we experienced that night. Going to the attendant's little house for tea and a wee dram finished a perfect evening.

If only the rest of the trip had turned out better for us all. The Northern Lighthouse Board calling for bids immediately upon our arrival was expected but their announcement that two other people had become interested in the property since last fall was frightening. At least we had left Stranraer before the bid opening.

You know we made the highest bid we could using all available resources. I remember standing in the Macdonalds' kitchen hearing the telephone ring, knowing it was the results and dreading to hear what our solicitor had to say. I kept hoping it just might be good news. It wasn't. The Board had accepted another bid. Our decision the preceding fall had been a mistake. In order to save a little money and be extra cautious we had lost a fabulous opportunity. I know I will regret that mistake for years and find myself playing the 'if only' game. There is no second chance with these bids so there is no 'if only'.

I know you were as disappointed as we were but hope the rest of the trip made up for the bad ending.

Frustrated,

Sharma

Date sent: Sunday, 23 April 1995
Subject: **Shoot Some More Arrows**
To: Susie@world.net

Susie,

Recovery from losing the Corsewall Point bidding has been slow. I keep wondering if we are foolish trying to do this. So many well meaning people have told us we were nuts it is hard not to believe it. Trying to buy lighthouse accommodations in Scotland is different but not crazy. I don't doubt the wisdom of what we are doing. I am more afraid of experiencing the hideous disappointment of having a bid rejected. The Corsewall failure is not something one risks again without worry. Now our choices are to continue looking for a lighthouse or think about a Scottish croft or a small farm on the ocean. Dean and I are even more certain after the time we spent at Corsewall that a lighthouse is what we want, so we are going to keep trying. I am again increasing my consulting to save more money for the 'lighthouse fund'.

Corsewall Point taught us the value of speed in securing this type of property. Lighthouses have become popular tourist businesses and holiday homes all over the world. It is critical to be the first on the scene with bid in hand. How to find what lighthouses are for sale is the big problem since we are so far away. My old boss use to say, 'If you shoot enough arrows you will eventually hit something'. We are going to shoot a lot of arrows and see if anything hits. Right now I need a source of information on potential properties.

Determined

Date sent: Monday, 24 April 1995
Subject: **A Source!**
To: Susie@world.net

Susie,

The Northern Lighthouse Board sent me a list of their properties that will be automated in the next three years. Most of the keepers' accommodations and land are to be sold after automation. Dean and I went over the list and picked the ones which fit our needs. We are scheduling trips so we will see them all before they come up for sale. If the Board suddenly calls for bids on a property we can submit one without a frantic trip to Scotland. Each trip must include many lighthouses, as transatlantic trips are expensive. We are considering a trip to Argyll and the Kintyre Peninsula. Ray and Marylou are interested in going with us. Would you like to join us? We could rent a self-catering house that looks out on the Inner Hebridean Islands. Next time when you come to the farm we can look at brochures and decide which self-catering house you like. I really like a house in a wee village called Mausdale. From there we could journey to the Mull of Kintyre Lighthouse and the Rinns of Islay, which are on our list of prime lighthouse candidates. Of course, it would not be all work. We could see a lot of beautiful countryside as well. The area is famous as it was near the Mull of Kintyre that St Columba arrived from Ireland in 574 AD, bringing Christianity to Scotland, and Somerled, buried at Saddell Abbey, overcame the Vikings to claim 'The Lordship of the Isles' to begin the epic saga of the reign of the MacDonalds. The site where Dunaverty Castle once stood marks the location of Scotland's forgotten, but most hideous massacre (far worse than Glencoe). In 1647 the Campbells under the Marquis of Argyll and Leslie's Covenanters finally ended the MacDonalds' influence in Kintyre. Marylou will have to be careful, as she is a Campbell, just in case any of those old resentments are still hanging around. It was at Campbeltown Cross that the Earl of Argyll initiated his unsuccessful rebellion against King James II. History and beautiful country, could we ask for anything more?

Have you ever heard Paul McCartney's song, 'The Mull of Kintyre'? If not, you should listen to it because that is what we should experience on this next trip.

Adventurer

Date sent: Wednesday, 13 September 1995
Subject: **Our House by the Sea**
To: sjk@world.net

Our little house by the sea turned out to be everything we had hoped. Out the front windows is the Sound of Jura and you can see the Inner Hebridean islands of Jura, Islay and Gigha. A small table and chairs in the front yard has become a favorite spot for having tea and drinks, as the view is out of this world. The sunsets are fantastic. The first night making dinner and watching the sunset I felt like I was in paradise.

Muasdale is a very small village and I was shocked the day after our arrival to go into the only shop to get the newspapers and have everyone say 'Hello' and know I was the American looking at the Mull of Kintyre lighthouse. We only told one person and all of sudden the entire neighborhood knew. In fact, even people outside the neighborhood. We visited a greenhouse and they knew us. The owners were related to the owners of the shop in Muasdale. That stop paid off as they gave us a fragrant pastel bouquet of sweet peas that is the centerpiece of our table.

We took a day off from lighthouses and visited the Isle of Gigha's stunning garden. After our stroll through the Achamore Gardens, with their beautiful tall rhododendrons plus some of the largest red poker plants I have ever seen, we had lunch at the Gigha Hotel where we were introduced to Gigha cheese, which is superb and comes in fruit flavors like pear and apple.

The other significant event was finding ripe brambles

(blackberries, as American call them) all around the house.
I made bramble scones and a cobbler, which was dark, sweet and juicy. In fact I made bramble scones twice.

The Muasdale Cook

Date sent: Thursday, 14 September 1995
Subject: **Mull of Kintyre**
To: sjk@world.net

Getting to the Mull of Kintyre lighthouse could have persuaded us lighthouses were not a place to retire. The road to the light-house is the narrowest and most twisting we have traveled in Scotland so far. Many times the roadside fell straight down hundreds of feet and, being single-track, we were constantly wondering if there was a vehicle coming around the bend.
It didn't help that we had rented a seven-passenger van to make the trip. At the car-park the surrounding hills were covered with purple heather and the lighthouse sat below with the ocean beyond. Inner Hebridean islands were dark bumps in the blue of the sea in the distance. It is a lovely spot if you have the courage to make the drive. Another even steeper, twisting road takes you to the lighthouse station itself. The Northern Lighthouse Board engineers were renovating the station, and the tower was wrapped in canvas and it was difficult to get pictures. We had tea with the two keepers who were to be made redundant within the year. Another benefit of going from one lighthouse to another is that we meet many of the last Northern Lighthouse Board keepers. They are remarkable people with tales of great adventure and devotion. (Some day I'll write a novel based on many of the stories they've shared.)

The head keeper at the Mull of Kintyre had shown incredible courage by searching the wreckage for survivors of a RAF heli-copter that crashed into the hill above the lighthouse. His efforts were unsuccessful since everyone was killed in the accident. The keeper has been nominated for an OBE for his bravery. I sure hope he gets it.

The Mull of Kintyre lighthouse is beautiful, sitting in the hills high above the ocean, but we decided it was not for us. Access is so challenging and all you can see away from the sea is an extremely ugly communications tower the Ministry of Defence has right beside the lighthouse and steep hills rising straight up like a large green wall.

Sharma (with one lighthouse down and many to go)

Date sent: Friday, 15 September 1995
Subject: **Islay**
To: sjk@world.net

We still have high hopes. Today we took the ferry to the island of Islay to look at lighthouse accommodations there. The Lords of Isles called Islay 'the jewel of the Hebrides' because of its extraordinary greenness and fertility. It reminded me a lot of Ireland.

Dean was particularly excited by this trip, since his definition of a perfect lighthouse is one located near seven of the world's best single malt distilleries. The distilleries in the south of the island – Lagavulin, Ardbeg and Laphroaig – produce the most strongly flavored whiskies in Scotland. The distilleries to the north – Bunnahabhain, Bowmore, Caol Ila and Bruichladdich tend to be of a lighter character; indeed some specify unpeated malt and draw their water direct from springs before it has had time to pick up much peat. In spite of this, they still taste peaty which is just fine with Dean.

The Rinns of Islay lighthouse station sits on Orsay Island at the end of a long narrow peninsula on the south-west corner of Islay. This station is dramatic with a tall lofty tower and can be seen from a great distance as you drive down the peninsula. Access is by small boat from Portnahaven, a beautiful town with pastel houses on a natural harbor at the end of the Rinns. The boat ride is only five minutes but getting into the boat is dangerous because the jetty is old and slippery. Access is one of the biggest problems encountered when shopping for a lighthouse.

Orsay Island is tiny and completely dominated by the magnificent 1825 Stevenson designed tower. The keepers took Dean up in the tower and he says he will never forget looking 'down' at three RAF jets flying in between the tower and Portnahaven. The keepers told us the RAF pilots like to use the lighthouses as a marker in their practice flights.

The Rinns of Islay has become my husband's first choice of all the Scottish lighthouse stations. He says the reason is the spectacular tower. I believe it is more an issue of being close to those distilleries and his love for single malt Scotch.

The Non-Scotch Drinker

Date sent: Tuesday, 19 September 1995
Subject: **Isle of Lewis**
To: sjk@world.net

Dean had to leave us after we left Argyll. Ray, Marylou and Sue and I went on from Loch Lomond in the 'Blue Chariot' better know as Skyeways Bus. Skyeways has been my method of getting to Skye since the trip when we were caught in the sheep jam. The buses are totally reliable, let me see the countryside, and drop me at a place that is easy for the Macdonalds to pick me up. The others wanted to travel around Skye so we left the Blue Chariot at Broadford to pick up a rental car. A small problem arose when the rental car that was supposed to have an automatic transmission turned out to have a straight shift. Since Marylou, our designated driver, had not driven a regular transmission in years we had a few rather jerky miles until she got the hang of it.

After a few days with the Macdonalds we took the ferry

from Uig to the Western Isles to look at the lighthouse at the Butt of Lewis. It takes 1 hour 45 minutes to cross the Minch on the ferry that brings you into Tarbert, the main village on Harris. We had quite a drive ahead of us because the Butt of Lewis is located on the far north-east corner of the island of Lewis near Ness. If we had taken the main route from Tarbert to Stornoway, which is only 37 miles on a good road, it would have been a pleasant trip. We decided to go out through the countryside only to find the landscape bleak and forlorn. My traveling companions took an immediate dislike to the Isle of Lewis feeling it was barren and reminded them of pictures they had seen of the moon's surface. The only interesting thing we saw was the Callanish Stones. Having seen Stonehenge I really enjoyed the freedom of walking close to the stones while being the only people there.

Ray, Marylou, and Sue disliked Lewis so much they wanted to leave immediately but having an appointment with the keeper of the Butt of Lewis the next day I wanted to stay. Finally they gave in and we all went to visit the Butt of Lewis. The Butt of Lewis lighthouse, built in 1863, has the only brick tower we have seen, exceptionally nice keepers' accommodations, effortless car access once you were on Lewis, and a beautiful setting. It went to the top of my list of possible purchases, even though it is known as the windiest place in Europe and my traveling companions disliked the area so much.

Windblown Sharma

Date sent: Thursday, 21 September 1995
Subject: **Northern Scotland**
To: Susie@world.net

Susie,

Hopefully you arrived home without any missed planes or other delays. Ray, Marylou and I are now in northern Scotland near

Thurso. You will be glad to know that our rental car is a BMW with an automatic transmission; a little different from the rental car we had on Skye. We are here to visit Strathy Point, Duncansby Head, Cape Wrath and Stroma lighthouse stations. We are staying at a secluded B&B located not too far from Strathy Point lighthouse. The wind picked up to gale force last night and was actually howling. It made me wonder if Northern Scotland was a place I wanted to live. The weather continued to get worse. We drove all the way to Durness to catch the ferry to Cape Wrath after I called the keepers who said it was a beautiful calm day at Cape Wrath. When we reached Durness the wind was too strong for the ferry and we had to turn around and drive back. Not a very successful trip by any means. We gave up on Stroma with the weather being so bad. Stroma is a short boat ride across the Pentland Firth. No one in his or her right mind goes into the Pentland Firth in a gale. We were able to reach Duncansby Head and Strathy Point stations although the wind was so strong my brother could not hold his camera still. Both of these properties were satisfactory for our needs but need repair. We notified the Northern Lighthouse Board we were interested. Neither are completely automated or on the market yet. We're just going to have to wait.

The Traveler

Date sent: Monday, 20 May 1996
Subject: **New Adventure – Scottish Radiance**
To: Susie@world.net

Susie,

It has been almost seven months since I have been in Scotland. My health is giving out with all this consulting and traveling. To get myself off the road I have initiated a new correspondence curriculum and hopefully that will keep the teaching income alive. My writing has been selling so I'll try and build up that part of my business to keep the 'lighthouse fund' growing without travel. I'm about to take on a new challenge. As I mentioned before I have been writing for an Internet magazine based in the Highlands of Scotland. A few weeks ago I got an offer from a website in the Outer Hebrides to start an Internet magazine for them. I would be the editor and web master. What a challenge this will be! The editing and writing is not a problem but the HTML programming is new field for me. I have already started the design and the first issue will be uploaded on 1 June. We are going to feature history, customs, Gaelic, and music – if I can ever make RealAudio work. Seven wonderful people have volunteered their time to write for me. Now I am really going to get a chance to share Scotland with the world.

A special column will be devoted to Scottish lighthouses. In my column 'Island Miniatures', I will share with the readers our search for a lighthouse home and maybe it will bring in some leads. Keep your fingers crossed, first that the magazine is a success, and second that it leads to good things in the lighthouse search.

Editor

Date sent: Wednesday, 19 March 1997
Subject: **Stardom on the** BBC
To: Susie@world.net

Two major news items with the first being that the Northern Lighthouse Board is getting ready to put Strathy Point Lighthouse on the market. You have not seen Strathy but it would be an acceptable choice. Problem is that the last time I saw it was a little run-down. I am off again to the northern coast of Scotland to check if Strathy's deterioration is continuing.

The really big news is that through Scottish Radiance, my Internet magazine, I have come to the attention of the BBC. Mark Rickards, a producer for BBC Scotland, has contacted me by e-mail and called a couple of times. He has decided to do a piece on our search for a Scottish lighthouse home and Scottish Radiance. I just knew Scottish Radiance would help me get in touch with more people about our quest. No better way to do it than the BBC!

Mark will travel with me for a few days, both videotaping my activities and interviewing me on audiotape. He has high hopes that, since we will be going to beautiful places, it will be a first-class television piece. The thought of being filmed by the BBC is terrifying!

Mark will be meeting me at Glasgow airport when I arrive from the US. This I could do without. I would have preferred to have him meet me in Thurso after I have an opportunity to get cleaned up after riding across the Atlantic all night on the plane. Jet lag will be a problem so I will probably be incoherent. He is convinced he wants to follow me from the beginning of the trip, including the bus ride to Thurso. This could be a disaster but it might help us get the word out that we are looking for a lighthouse home.

Speaking of that night flight across the Atlantic, I am starting to hate it. I try to get as much sleep as possible but they keep pestering you with drinks, meals, and movies. If I go to sleep right after they serve dinner I might get four hours rest before it is time for breakfast. By the way, I tried to count the number of times I have flown to Scotland in the last few years and I can't remember. The number is too high. When I get on that eastbound plane across the Atlantic and try to sleep, I almost agree with all of our critics. This search for a lighthouse is nuts.

The Soon-to-be Worst BBC *Feature*

Date sent: Tuesday, 4 April 1997
Subject: **New Solicitor**
To: Susie@world.net

Susie,

I have hired a new solicitor via e-mail. Dean and I thought it
might be wise to have a solicitor in Northern Scotland since it
looks like a bid for Strathy Point is in the works. I am finding it
a little unsettling to have a solicitor I have not met. The solicitors we had in the south-west did such a good job on the
Corsewall Point bid. We lost but it definitely was not their fault.
I've set up a meeting with the new solicitor on the upcoming trip
so I can identify a person with the name.

One good thing has occurred from hiring the new solicitor;
he had information on another lighthouse that is for sale. Noss
Head Lighthouse, built in 1849 and engineered by Alan
Stevenson, located near Wick on the east coast of Scotland.
According to my lighthouse book the light in the eighteen meter
high tower flashes red with a range of twenty one miles and
white with a range of twenty five miles. The station was
automated in 1987 but the keepers' accommodations have
apparently not fared well under private ownership. The sad story
of Noss Head was common knowledge. Noss Head keepers'
accommodations have an absentee owner who has only visited
one or twice in the entire time he has owned the property. Being
just a short distance from town, vandals have torn the dwellings
to pieces. I have been told the accommodations are a wreck.
Evidently the Board succeeded in getting the owner to sell the
property since he was not keeping the maintenance covenant. I
am sure I have mentioned this before, but when anyone buys
lighthouse property where the Northern Lighthouse Board still
owns the tower you sign a covenant that you will maintain the
property up to the Board's standards.

I am going visit Noss Head and to see whether, if we offer a
low purchase price, we can afford to renovate it.

In many ways I dread paying a visit to Noss Head. I have seen enough lighthouses in the final days of a slow horrible death here in Michigan. Each one just breaks my heart.

Also, I am more than a little apprehensive about hiring a solicitor over the Internet.

Uneasy Sharma

Date sent: Tuesday, 24 June 1997
Subject: **Thurso and Noss Head**
To: Susie@world.net

Mark Rickards met me at the Glasgow airport and he was not kidding about shooting everything. First came the bus ride from Glasgow to Thurso. I felt no anxiety related to the camera since I have appeared on television many times, and produced and appeared in seven instructional video programs. But, I must admit it was unsettling being filmed on a bus after being up all night flying across the Atlantic. I wonder if anything I said made any sense.

The morning after we arrived in Thurso we met with the bank manager I was using in the area. It was amazing to see how some people react to the name BBC, and even more so to a video camera. Some of the people were comfortable with the camera while others refused to be filmed or audio-taped. One thing for sure, we drew a lot of attention as Mark followed me down the street with the camera rolling. I bet everyone in Thurso thought I was some visiting celebrity.

It was a perfect day with no clouds and a slight breeze. We used the same taxi driver Dean and I had hired on previous trips to take us to the Thurso area lighthouses. He was uncomfortable at first being filmed and recorded, but he quickly rose to the task, becoming relaxed and informative. We met Steve Dailly, an administrator for Northern Lighthouse Board, at Strathy Point, who showed us around. The property is continuing to deteriorate but has great potential. We should make a bid for it. After Strathy we went to Duncansby Head where the main house was still occupied but the two assistant keepers' houses could be seen. Duncansby Head is not my favorite of the accommodations I've seen but it could work as a last resort. Asbestos problems have to be corrected before it could be marketed.

One of the most exciting events of the Thurso trip for me occurred at Duncansby Head. The BBC producer, taxi driver and I walked a short distance to see the famous pointed Duncansby Stacks. On the way we passed a cliff that was home to hundreds of puffins, a bird I had always wanted to see in the wild. Like most people who see puffins for the first time I was amazed how tiny they are. I expected to see something the size of a penguin but was shocked to see something half that size living on the cliffs far above the sea. Naturally out came the camera so Mark could get me making friends with the puffins. I decided that it would be real asset if the lighthouse we finally purchase was near a puffin colony.

After Strathy Point and Duncansby Head we headed for Wick and Noss Head. Mark and I parted for the night as he was meeting another BBC staff member, who would help us film Noss Head, at a different hotel. The next morning I was shocked when they pulled up in a convertible with the top down. It was the first convertible I had ever seen in Scotland with its top down, since it rains at lot. The Scottish weather did not let us down as it began to rain on us before we arrived at the lighthouse.

I dreaded seeing Noss Head since I knew how badly it had been damaged. The property is beautifully set, surrounded by ocean with a castle ruin just down the bay, but when we got closer to the buildings we could see the houses with no windows and walls that had been ripped apart. It was dreadful.

Steve Dailly from the Northern Lighthouse Board arrived and offered to take us up into the tower. By then it was raining hard and the wind was roaring. Being in a lighthouse tower in a strong wind is a weird experience. The wind screams as it batters the tower. Some of the best footage Mark got was inside Noss Head's tower with the wind and rain echoing around our heads. The worst was probably my interview in front of the lighthouse where I had to hold on to the wall to keep my balance and try to speak above the roaring wind.

I'm going to suggest to Dean that we make an offer on Noss Head. The property would be absolutely perfect and even has twenty acres plus steading for Dean's cows. The big unknown is the cost of the needed renovations on the two vandalized houses. We might be able to afford the renovations if the price for the property was reduced.

On My Way to Lewis,
Sharma

Date sent: Friday, 27 June 1997
Subject: **Birthday at Edinbane**
To: Susie@world.net

Sue

I said goodbye to Mark whom I had come to like very much even with all the pressure of the filming. I headed toward Stornoway to meet with Scott Hatton, Scottish Radiance's technical genius.

Scott met me at the ferry terminal and we went out for dinner at a nice Stornoway hotel which served excellent fresh Isle of Lewis fish. A nice beginning to celebrating my birthday that was the next day. Scott and I did some work on the magazine that evening at the offices of Eolas, the magazine's home. This was a special treat for the editor who lives 'across the pond'.

27 June – my birthday, Scott took me out to the Butt of Lewis lighthouse for an inspection. The trip may have convinced him I wasn't totally insane wanting to live at a lighthouse station, isolated and surrounded by ocean and birds. He has always been a little skeptical about my lighthouse 'thing'. The

visit to Stornoway was short as I planned to catch the Skye ferry in order to return to what I consider my first Scottish home, Orbost Farm, for my 'real' birthday celebration. The plan for this evening was for Robert and Margaret to choose a place we could all go (including the girls) to have dinner for my birthday.

When I saw the Macdonalds at Skye's Uig ferry port, I knew I had arrived 'home'. It wasn't until that moment that I realized how rushed and nervous I felt with the lighthouse inspections and the BBC. I climbed into the back seat with Sarah on one side and Jenny on the other and relaxed. Needless to say it wasn't peaceful as we were all trying to catch up with each other's activities. It had been four months since we had been together. We were so busy talking I didn't even notice the beautiful hills of Skye as they rushed by the window.

The Macdonalds had chosen a hotel for dinner. The Edinbane Hotel is in the wee village of Edinbane near Dunvegan. The hotel had new owners who had completely renovated the place since the last time I had been there. The bar and dining room were now very light and cheerful with huge glass windows with Scottish thistle stained glass inserts. Our table was bathed in the late evening sun. The adults ordered wine with the girls having Cokes and the non-stop conversation continued. In fact, we were so slow in ordering our meal that the girls reminded us we came here to eat. As we ate a superb dinner, some people began bringing in a lot of 'stuff'. Soon we realized the 'stuff' was musical instruments and a band was going to play that night. The girls were thrilled. The group began playing about the time I was finishing an outstanding Scottish trifle for my pudding.

It was an enchanted moment. I was on the Isle of Skye with dear friends listening in person to some of my favorite Celtic music. Up to this point most of my listening to Celtic music was by radio or CD. You could not have asked for a more perfect birthday, except that I would have liked Dean to be with us. The audience was all local people. I was easily identified as the only tourist with my 'US Lighthouse Keepers' sweatshirt. The assembly included someone who brought back unpleasant memories: the owner of Neist Point lighthouse who bought it before we had a chance to make an offer, was standing at the bar. I found myself envying him.

The audience both listened and danced. The girls and I frolicking (you couldn't really call it dancing) on the dance floor even brought applause from other members of the audience. What made it so special was that it was just a very good local Celtic band playing for a room of friends and neighbors. This American was very lucky to celebrate her birthday in such a delightful way.

A Year Older,
Sharma

Date sent: Friday, 25 July 1997
Subject: **Absolute Disaster**
To: Susie@world.net

Sue,

You will never believe what has happened – total complete disaster. I still find it hard to believe that we could get into such a mess. Returning to the USA I began to develop an offer for the Noss Head lighthouse accommodations. I contacted architects and Historic Scotland to evaluate the renovations necessary. Our survey set the value at £36,000. The owner agreed with the evaluation and immediately called for bids.

Our bid was submitted and, after much confusion we were informed our bid was rejected with no reason given.

I feel our only hope of securing a Scottish lighthouse is through the Northern Lighthouse Board. To be honest I feel we should just give up this lighthouse nonsense.

Dejected and Defeated,
Sharma

Date sent: Friday, 26 September 1997
Subject: **Discouraged**
To: Susie@world.net

After the unsuccessful bid for Noss Head I find it's difficult to maintain any interested in buying a Scottish lighthouse. We have been at it for six years, spent thousands of dollars and have nothing to show except frustration. Those who think we are nuts are right. It is too big a dream for our limited resources. Each failed bid seems to hurt more.

If we had been looking for a lighthouse fifteen years ago our chances would have been better. When the Northern Lighthouse Board first started selling the automated stations' keepers' accommodations there was a bigger selection and the price was low. Some of the most beautiful lighthouses were sold very early in the process. Now only a few good ones are left. A resale, like Noss Head, is still possible but our biggest problem is how to find out about a potential resale. This weekend we will sit down and discuss buying a small croft or a house by the sea.

I am maintaining contact with the Northern Lighthouse Board since they still have a couple of potential properties left. Strathy Point is bogged down in an argument between local crofters and the Northern Lighthouse Board over the access road to the lighthouse. Duncansby Head still has asbestos problems, and the pipes froze last winter so now the building has water damage.

Thanks for taking the time to let me cry on your shoulder. I am just tired and discouraged at this point. Sometimes I wish I had never heard of Scotland or lighthouses. The only thing we accomplish is spending more time and money, without getting any closer to what we want.

I Hate Lighthouses,
Sharma

Date sent: Sunday, 28 September 1997
Subject: **Trip To Scotland**
To: Susie@world.net

Sue,

Dean and I discussed the whole 'lighthouse situation' and have
decided to wait and see what happens. We are going to Scotland
in January to visit the Macdonalds but will not visit any lighthouses. It'll seem strange to not go anywhere near lighthouses.
Maybe this time we will have a vacation and enjoy Scotland like
we used to be before we started this insane lighthouse search.

On Vacation,
Sharma

Date sent: Saturday, 31 January 1998
Subject: **Just to say Hi!**
To: Susie@world.net

Susie,

We just returned from Scotland and the trip was a nice change.
Nothing new has occurred on the lighthouse front. For seven
years we have been devoting time, energy and money to finding
a Scottish home. You have to give us credit for one thing. We are
not quitters. Strathy Point should come on the market next year.
Since we have devoted so much time and money to that particular piece of property we will probably follow up with a bid. For
some reason Strathy just does not excite me any more.

Getting turned down is the norm these days, so I think I can
handle one more rejection if there is any chance at all.

Cynical,
Sharma

Date sent: Sunday, 4 October 1998
Subject: **Corsewall Resale and South-west Scotland**
To: Susie@world.net

Sue,

My contact at the Lighthouse Board notified me the Strathy
Point dispute over the road access has been resolved and they are
ready to put the property on the market. So I'm back in
Scotland. My main reason for coming is to meet with Rob
Blackwell, publishing manager of Appletree Press, for whom I
am writing *Scotland – A Complete Guide and Road Atlas* and a
book on Scottish lighthouses. Rob and I met in Stranraer as the
ferry arrives directly there from Belfast where Appletree Press is
located.

   Guess what? A few days after we arranged to meet in
Stranraer, Corsewall Point came back on the market. I think you
once predicted that would happen. The lighthouse has been
turned into a luxury hotel and seems to be doing very well. Dean
and I decided to take another look and see whether it is worth
the almost £900,000 asking price. It is unlikely we could take
that much of risk. Only a few years ago we worried about risk-
ing £100,000 on Corsewall Point.

   The bankers recommend that we do not even consider purchasing unless there is a significant drop in asking price. Rob
and I had lunch at the hotel. Elegant hotels are great. What they
have done to Corsewall just did not fit an historic lighthouse.
I keep wondering how they got the planning variances to make
the changes. It is all irrelevant as the owner would not even consider dropping the price.

   The sun was shining brilliantly on the waters of Loch Ryan
the day after we visited Corsewall Point. It really did not seem
possible this was Scotland in October since the weather has been
fair. Today Rob and I headed into northern Galloway to find a
boat to Ailsa Craig Lighthouse, located on an island just off of
the Girvan coast. After Ailsa Craig we wanted to investigate

Turnberry Lighthouse. According to my lighthouse book
Turnberry Lighthouse was built in 1873 and automated in 1986.
Its tower has a range of 24 miles and flashes every 15 seconds,
and is supposed to be beautiful.

Driving north discussing the delightful weather, I studied the
map trying to figure out how you navigate through Turnberry
Golf Course to the lighthouse. There is a small road shown on
the map. It goes directly through the course. Cars on Turnberry
Golf Course are probably frowned upon. After much discussion
we decided we would ask, and hope someone would tell us how
to reach the lighthouse. I had not thought to get written
permission to visit the light from the Northern Lighthouse Board
so they will just have to believe that we have it.

Since the tourist season is over we found no boat to Ailsa
Craig at Girvan. I cheerfully announced, 'Well, that will give us
more time to have coffee and shortbread at Turnberry'.

Everybody knows about Turnberry Golf Course because of
the British Open. Since I don't play golf the course is not the
reason I like Turnberry. Food is Turnberry's appeal for me.
Visiting Turnberry Golf Course for shortbread and coffee has
been a tradition ever since my first visit to Stranraer four years
ago. Remember how we sat and looked at the snow on the tops
of Arran mountains as we sipped their wonderful coffee. This is
the first time I will attempt to get close to the lighthouse. I have
always been afraid I would be kicked off of the golf course
trying to get to it. I am more positive this time about inspecting
Turnberry Lighthouse since I have permission from the Northern
Lighthouse Board to visit this station.

Turnberry Golf Course is still an elegant and beautiful place.
I might just take up golf so I can wander around Turnberry's
beautiful grounds. The hotel facility is first class. The second you
enter you sense you should be wearing an evening gown instead
of jeans and a sweatshirt. Never having been shy, I led the way
and Rob and I strolled in with all of those rich people. My last
visit I had purchased a beautiful shirt for half price at the gift shop

so first thing we checked to see if they had any bargains. But, alas no bargains were to be found this time. The sweatshirt I wanted was $80! So much for that, we headed for the dining room.

Windows looking out over the golf course to the sea, Ailsa Craig, Isle of Arran, and the lighthouse in the distance are on three sides of dining room. I always select a table that allows me to face the lighthouse since it is stunning with the green links in front of it. As we entered, Rob overheard someone remark they had just gotten Michael Douglas's autograph along with two other stars. We started watching everyone who came in hoping to see someone famous. The week before a pro-celebrity tournament had been held at St Andrews. The participants must be making the rounds of the great Scottish courses which explained the three helicopters we saw sitting at the edge of the course as we drove up.

We ordered coffee and shortbread while discussing how to get out to the lighthouse since we had not seen the road marked on the map. When the waiter brought our order, told him I had permission to visit the lighthouse but did not know how to reach it. Without hesitation he gave directions and reminded us the lighthouse building was closed. We assured him we only wanted to get near to take pictures. I am amazed how easy it was.

Since we were off to the lighthouse I breezed right by the gift shop on the way out without second thoughts. The road was not easy to find but once we found it was just a short drive to the car-park. Then, you walk across the course to reach the lighthouse. It did not help to know the golfers hitting balls toward us were pros and celebrities. We managed to reach a small modern building standing just outside the lighthouse gate without injury from flying golf balls. It was a bar so the golfers can get a drink on the back-side of the course. Why not – after all this was Turnberry!

Turnberry Lighthouse is beautifully set but sadly neglected. Most first floor windows are covered with boards but the ones on the second floor were open to the elements. Piles of rubble surrounding the building were perhaps coming from the inside through the open windows. We could only imagine what the condition inside the lighthouse must be. The lighthouse was such a sad contrast to the elegant golf course and its buildings.

Depressed, I sat on the grass inside the keeper's walled garden where I could only see the lighthouse and hear the sea.

I found peace and serenity by forgetting the golf course with all of its riches while Rob was off taking pictures. I watched the clouds drift by the tower. Protected inside the garden by a beautiful old stone wall, Rob and I relaxed with the beautiful lighthouse, the sea and the past. While sitting in the garden I happened to mention to Rob that Eshaness Lighthouse accommodations on the Shetland Islands had come on the market. (Dean and I had not even considered Eshaness when the Northern Lighthouse Board had mentioned it to us because it was so far north.) I will always remember Rob's reaction of absolute shock and then excitement. He had been to Eshaness when he lived in the Shetlands. He thought Eshaness was one of the most beautiful places in the world. He said we were making a big mistake not to at least go see it. I promised him I would go in January when we returned to Scotland if we did not buy Strathy Point.

Rob wanted to go into Ayr to see if we could find an Ordnance Survey on Eshaness or some pictures, so we left the tranquility of the garden. Once again we began the life-threatening walk across the golf course. Suddenly Rob drew my attention to someone who was driving a ball our way. Stopping we waited until the golfer was finished before walking again. As the golfer approached and greeted us I had the feeling I've seen him before. I knew he was a movie star but we could not remember his name. It was not until later that night that we realized the man who was so friendly was Morgan Freeman, a well-known actor. I do not know why it surprised me so much to see him, after all we were on the world famous Turnberry Golf Course.

The answer to why I was surprised is easy. For me Turnberry is not thought of as a golf course. In my mind it is only the home of the best coffee and shortbread in south-west scotland and the appalling place where a beautiful lighthouse is being allowed to die surrounded by opulence.

I am on my way to Strathy Point to see what condition it is after another year of being abandoned.

One of the Turnberry Celebrities,
Sharma
Date sent: Friday, 9 October 1998
Subject: **Strathy Point for the Fifth Time**
To: Susie@world.net

After I left Rob I returned to Strathy Point AGAIN. Except for the possible resale of Eshaness, Strathy looks like our only hope for a Scottish lighthouse. When I met with the Northern Lighthouse Board staff in Edinburgh they indicated that Strathy's roof was beginning to fall in. Dean felt if that was happening we should have it surveyed immediately to see if it was worth repairing. Every time I return to Strathy I am devastated by the amount of damage that has occurred since the last trip. The trips are never more than six months apart so you would think it would not be so noticeable. I still cannot get over how fast lighthouses can deteriorate if they are not maintained. The sea is brutal on their physical structure. The surveyor thought that the ceiling plaster coming down in the entryway was not a major concern. He valued the property at only £60,000, which I thought was reasonable for three houses. He felt Strathy's isolation and the sixty steps that have to be climbed to reach the houses decreased the value of the property.

We will submit a bid in the near future, which may nudge the Board to place the property up for public bid. Why not submit one more bid. After all the trips to Strathy we should at least go that far.

I doubt that the bid will be accepted but if we don't try we will never know. Am I beginning to sound negative?

Sharma

Date sent: Friday, 9 October 1998
Subject: **Fantastic Shetland Islands**
To: Susie@world.net

Dear Sue,

How would you like to come to Scotland with us to see Strathy
Point lighthouse and then go to the Shetland Islands to visit
Eshaness Lighthouse in January? Don't let the fact that the
Shetlands are so far north they have to be put into a box in the
upper right-hand corner of maps of Scotland scare you. It is a
long way up there, but listen to what I found in the Shetland
Island Tourist Board brochure:

*'If you want to get away from it all then Shetland is for you.
As close to Norway as it is to Scotland, Shetland is rugged and
remote. Its natural, raw beauty, its unique identity and culture, a
surfeit of nature and wildlife, and warmth of welcome, will fill
up your senses and overwhelm you.*

*Shetland has over one hundred islands, bordered by jagged
cliffs and bleached white beaches, and peppered with sea inlets.
Shetland is ruled by water. On a fair day the sea is a paintbox
turquoise, merging to cobalt as it becomes deeper. If the weather
breaks, the force of the boiling surging ocean – which has sculpt-
ed the islands' charismatic coastline – is equally impressive.*

*The purity of the air and water provides a haven for wildlife,
sea-life and bird-life. The sound of the birds is ever present. From
screaming gulls to dive-bombing great skuas, and from huge
gannets to charming cartoon-like puffins, there's a plethora of birds,
including the rarities for which the Shetland Islands are famous.*

*Rich in history and heritage Shetland has derived much of its
culture from the Vikings, although Neolithic and Iron Age
remains speak of a past long before that.*

*The charm of Shetland invades all the senses: the smells of
the sea or the wildflowers, which proliferate everywhere, or the
peat smoke from welcoming fires, the sounds of the sea, birds,
sheep and nature, the toe-tapping Shetland fiddle music and*

sing-song accent of the locals, the awe-inspiring views and the bracing clear air from the cliff tops, the elation after outdoor activity; the superb taste of the food – all kinds of fish and seafood (caught locally of course), world acclaimed lamb with its distinctive heathery flavour, and not forgetting indigenous Shetland dishes, including restit mutton and piltocks.

Time seems to slow down in Shetland, where space and tranquility become soothing balms for life's pressures, and activity is dictated by choice. Shetland gives you the space you want the time you need'.

It sounds too good to miss. Even though Dean and I might be submitting a bid for Strathy, we should go to the Shetlands. We might not ever get another chance.

Sharma
Shetland Bound

Date sent: Thursday, 19 November 1998
Subject: **Why Lighthouses?**
To: Susie@world.net

Susie,

Whoopee! I just had an article accepted by *Lighthouse Digest*, the International Lighthouse Magazine. I am not sure you will be able to find a copy so here is what I said.

Why Lighthouses?

Not often do I stop to measure why something matters in my life unless someone asks or something brings it to my attention. Recently an e-mail slipped into my list with the title, 'Lighthouse'. Almost compulsive about answering my e-mail, especially those with the title 'Lighthouse', I read it at once. It was from a reader in Ireland who loves lighthouses.

He asked me the question, 'Why lighthouses?' I wanted to flippantly declare, 'Why not?' except the writer is a lighthouse aficionado searching for an explanation for his fascination as well as my own. In my usual hasty e-mail style I dashed off a list of words which I associate with lighthouses as an answer. The question haunted me and to preserve my sanity it merited a complete answer. So here, Rob, and all of the other lighthouse lovers who might read this column, is a more comprehensive answer.

First, lighthouses are ordinarily found in remote areas with a small number of human neighbors. The nearest human beings to Neist Point, which I have visited many times, are a 45-minute walk away! Most Scottish lighthouses' only neighbors are sheep. Many facilities can only be approached by boat, so I guess their neighbors are fish.

My first reason, not necessarily the most important, is their remote location where I can be completely alone. At this time in my life that is a necessity since my life is hectic, full of deadlines and an assortment of chaos. I have a compulsion to be surrounded by nature, but isolated where I can think and feel nothing if I like.

Second, all of the stations' postal addresses could be 'Ocean Place' as their relationship with the sea is an intimate one. Some are found on peninsulas surrounded on three sides by water. Others on top of lofty heads look across miles of ocean. 'Flat land lights' are situated where one can walk out as the door and within a few feet be on the shore. Rock stations are usually the only buildings on small islands where access is by boat. The air surrounding a lighthouse is fresh with the smell of the sea. The melody of the waves touching the shore is often the only sound you hear. Like classical music, the waves can be violent and loud or soft and peaceful. A valid reason for someone like me who lives on a farm surrounded by pastures is that they are a stone throw from the ocean. Our farm is beautiful, but I continually yearn for the sea.

If you are a nature lover, then a lighthouse is one of the best places in the world to experience ocean creatures in their natural *environment. I have witnessed dolphins, whales, many different types of sea-birds including puffins, and seals within a short distance of many keepers' houses. My favorites are the seals, which at most Scottish lighthouses can be seen through the windows playing outside on the rocks. Good fishing is a few feet beyond the house and there is nothing better than a lobster you have caught over the side of the lighthouse wall. Being close enough to a whale to hear the blow is sufficient reason for me to love all lighthouses.*

The lighthouses are a part of history. If the towers could talk, they would relate an extraordinary saga of man and his ongoing relationship with the sea. They could tell of the tragedies and triumphs that have occurred in the world of water that surrounds them. Tales of the courageous and devoted keepers who kept the lights blazing, or tragic stories of death and shipwrecks are forever chiseled in their hard stone exterior. Most of the lighthouses are historic buildings, some dating back to the 1700s.

Many perceive lighthouse buildings as physically beautiful. Surrounded by exquisite locations, the nature of their architecture leads to feelings of majesty. The tall towers stretch out to touch the sky while brilliant beacons pierce into the black of the night. Even the Fresnel lenses during the daytime look like magnificent gold diamonds sitting in their towers with the light streaming through them to paint rainbows of color on the ground below. For many lighthouse buffs beauty is the main reason they cherish these structures.

Lighthouses, due to changes in technology, have in many places become unnecessary. They have gone from being lovingly tended by their keepers to the cold reality of being operated by machines through phone lines. Thank goodness, in Scotland the lights are still shining and the properties maintained. In many parts of the world, the lights have been shut off and the properties abandoned. We once had 247 lighthouses on the Great Lakes, but now we have less than one hundred in good condition. Tears come to my eyes when I think of something as historic and beautiful as Scotland's Duncansby Head being allowed to die a slow and hideous death. At least I know the Northern Lighthouse Board will not allow that to happen to Duncansby. If the property cannot be saved, they will destroy it quickly and finally. I relate this to how I feel when I know a good friend might die and the time we have left becomes so very valuable.

Having now given you some of the intellectual reasons, I want to close with an emotional moment in my life which brings it all together:

Snow was gently falling as we drove to the lonely peaceful parking lot a few hundred feet from Corsewall Point Light. Having had dinner with Tom Kelly, the occasional keeper for Corsewall, we were on our way to his house for a cup of tea, but had made a short detour wanting to see the lighthouse up close in full night-time operation. Walking to a rocky viewpoint where the only sound was the crashing sea below us, we looked back at the lighthouse. The beacon striking out from the tower was revolving in the snow. The light made long rays of silver narrow at the beginning and wider the further from the tower they penetrated the sky. Framed in the beam of light was the glitter of hundreds of twinkling speckles caused by the ice crystals. I once related this scene in another of my published stories to the blades of a helicopter revolving in the night. That is an accurate description of their appearance.

As I wrote this article I remembered that night and realized to me it answered the question 'Why Lighthouses?' The beacon illuminating the snow was alone in the sky, continuing to keep the ships at sea safe, creating another moment of history among the hundreds of such moments since the lighthouse was built. Surrounded by the sounds of the sea that instant belonged only to the four of us. I got back in the car, snowflakes mixing with my tears of wonderment, with a deep feeling of total serenity. That is the best answer to 'Why Lighthouses?' I can think of, and its memory will stay with me forever.

Well how did I do? Do you think I answered the question?

The Author

Date sent: Monday, 16 November 1998
Subject: **Eshaness, Can It Be Real?**
To: Susie@world.net

Susie,

I have been studying the particulars of Eshaness Lighthouse keepers' accommodations. On paper the house sounds perfect and just the right size for two people! The main house includes a sitting room with flame-effect fire insert in a tiled fireplace with wood mantelpiece and trimming. There is a big walk-in cupboard and an additional wall heater. The dining room has a deep red coal-burning Rayburn Royal that heats the water. There is another electric wall heater in this room plus two windows that have custom-made sun blinds. The kitchen has new pale oak cabinets with large storage spaces. By the window to the south is a Shanks traditional sink with two compartments – one deep, one standard. Included in the sale are a new electric cooker with extractor hood, a Whirlpool refrigerator with oak finish and a Bosch freezer. The kitchen has a supplementary floor level electric room heater. Behind the kitchen is a utility room with plumbing for dishwasher and automatic washing machine. The bathroom is tiled with pale decorative tiling. A new Indian Ivory Standard suite has been added. Heating in the bathroom includes a heated towel rail and additional electric heater, plus an exhaust fan. The master bedroom has a fireplace and wall heater plus a large cupboard and walk-in closet. The second bedroom has an open fireplace, storage cupboard and another wall heater. A unique feature of this room is a wood and brass mounted electronic weather station with a dial made from a Spitfire airplane.

In addition the old generator house has been made into three rooms. An office with a gallery with pine planking, extensive storage space, shelving, and wall heater. A tool storage area is in the middle of the three rooms. The last room is a workshop with a large workbench. There is a freestanding garage with heater, storage, and external night disturbance light. Wow, it has everything we would ever need.

You can drive up to the front door. No steps to contend with (unlike Strathy Point) is a real asset for people who are considering it for their old age. Being just one house, if the price is right we might not have to operate it as a self-catering business in order to support it. Eshaness is the first accommodation we have come across in all of the time we have been looking at Scottish lighthouses that is being sold almost completely renovated.

I have always wanted an Aga or Rayburn stove but when I priced them in the US they were too costly. You've seen them. They are heavy cast iron with a heat source on one side and two ovens on the other. The top can be used just like the burners on our stovetops. The Shetland solicitor that is representing the sellers says the Rayburn is used for supplementary heat, hot water, and cooking. If the electricity expires you can survive comfortably by living in the room with the stove. Many Shetlanders like them because they can burn peat in the stove, and Shetland has lots of peat.

Dean is still not as positive about Eshaness as I am. The Shetland Islands are at the end of the earth near the North Pole is his usual comment. It is a long way up there and getting back and forth might be a problem. Actually, I think his biggest concern is getting stranded up there and not being able to get back to the States in a timely manner. My lighthouse book says the Eshaness Lighthouse engineer was David A. Stevenson. This is a plus as far as Dean is concerned since from the beginning he wanted to live in a facility designed by the world's greatest lighthouse engineering family.

The Strathy Point bid seems to be jammed up in red tape so we are definitely going to the Shetlands to look at Eshaness in January. I am glad we decided to fly to Shetland and take the ferry back so we can get a feel for both types of transportation. Dean wanted me to warn you that, since we are going near the North Pole, you should bring plenty of warm clothes.

Encouraged
Sharma

Date sent: Tue, 8 December 1998
Subject: **Fuming!**
To: Susie@world.net

Sue,

It takes a lot to get me extremely angry but anger is too tame a word for what I am feeling now. Rage is a more appropriate term. We submitted a bid to the Northern Lighthouse Board for Strathy Point right after I got back from Scotland in October. It took forever to get an answer from them. They put our bid on the table, what ever that means, as they still had some details to complete. We kept getting promises that the public bid opening would happen in the near future. I have a file full of faxes with excuses why the sale was not proceeding. The solicitor and I are baffled. We submitted a bid for full survey value and we were the only interested party. Even taking into consideration that they had to follow internal procedures it makes no sense taking so long. The whole process is stuck. Our solicitor is furious but, to give him credit, he is hanging in there. The Northern Lighthouse Board staff are not answering our messages. Communication has completely broken down.

I have always felt that the Lighthouse Board employees we have been working with all these years were our friends. When will I ever learn you should not mix business with friendship? Ever since we submitted our bid for Strathy Point the relationship with the Board has been different. Hopefully when this is all over we can go back to where we were.

Today I faxed the Northern Lighthouse Board Chief Executive Officer trying to get some clarification. Our solicitor is trying to contact the Board's solicitors to see if he can give us any information. It is doubtful we will know anything related to Strathy Point before we leave for Scotland and that means our itinerary will include a short visit to Strathy Point and then on to the Shetlands.

I am getting excited about seeing the Shetlands as they are a place I have always wanted to visit but never had the opportunity. I love new adventures.

Heading North,
Sharma

Date sent: Saturday, 9 January 1999
Subject: **Strathy Point for the Sixth Time**
To: rampaint@world.net

Ray and Marylou,

Dean, Sue and I arrived in Thurso without a problem. Dean and I have been here so much it is beginning to feel like home. It will be fun to show the area to Susie since this is her first trip. Things have changed since the last trip. The hotel where we always stay has been remodeled and is elegant. Our old reliable taxi driver had a heart attack and we had to find a new one. The new young taxi driver we found is super. Thurso must have oodles of great taxi companies or we have just been lucky in our choices.

We were shocked by the condition of Strathy Point. The roof had started to leak, doors had rusted shut, the entrances to the assistant keeper's houses were impassable and some of the windows were broken. Strathy Point is dying a slow hideous death sitting empty for over two years.

Sue and Dean felt we should not pursue Strathy Point any further. Renovation costs would drive our overall cost too high. I know they are right but I just don't want to admit it. Thank goodness we have tickets to Shetland to look at Eshaness Lighthouse. After all of the hurt and disappointment I still do not want to give up. Each time I visit a lighthouse I see myself living there and it thrills me. I am a stubborn person but we are running out of options. I am tired of the struggle. A quote from my former partner rings in my head. 'After hitting your head against a stone wall for years it feels so good when you finally quit'. If Eshaness does not work I'll have to give in to common sense and give it up. I think Dean already has.

Discouraged,
Sharma

Date sent: Tuesday, 12 January 1999
Subject: **Ice and Airplanes**
To: rampaint@world.net

Ray and Marylou,

Dean feels any lighthouse in the Shetlands would be difficult to reach from the USA and just to prove him right the weather delayed our Shetland arrival. The morning we were to leave an ice storm hit the northern part of Scotland. Luckily the ice on the road melted so our reliable taxi driver was able to get us to the Wick airport. We left early because of the weather so we were able to make a short side trip to let Sue and Dean could see Noss Head, near the airport. It made me feel good to see that renovations had been started.

At the airport we found many frustrated travelers, as no planes had been able to land all morning. The reservation desk clerk said our plane was on its way so we felt confident we would not have any delays. Not true! The plane flew right over the airport and continued on its way to Sumburgh. We were left in Wick. After a long argument with the reservation people we had to accept that we were not going to get out of Wick by plane. The only option was to go south using ground transportation and see if we could get a plane. Taking a taxi we went to the bus station only to find out we had missed the last bus of the day. We then went to the train station. The only train departing that afternoon which was going near a major airport was to Inverness. Insane as it sounds we took the train in the exact opposite direction we wanted to go. Arriving late in Inverness we were relieved that the Station Hotel had a room for us. The next morning we went to the airport early to see if we could get a plane to the Shetlands. We finally departed for the Shetlands after a long delay because of gales.

The weather was not helping make Shetland look like a good place to buy a home. Dean just might be right. The Shetlands are at the end of the earth and too hard to reach. I am afraid he will just turn down Eshaness on that fact alone.

The Tired Traveler,
Sharma

Date sent: Tuesday, 12 January 1999
Subject: **Shetland Island and the Ponies**
To: rampaint@world.net

Ray and Marylou,

The Shetland Islands were a huge surprise. The islands lie as close to Norway as they do to Scotland. About twenty years ago when the North Sea oil reserves became big business Shetland changed from a remote crofting and fishing community to a more fast-paced and up-to-date area. It seems to be a wonderful mix of the old and the new. The airport bustles with hundreds of helicopters flying back and forth to the oil fields. Most major roads are two lanes and well taken care of.

One of the things I wanted to see was a wild Shetland pony. It's small size and thick coat are adaptations to the Shetland climate.

The ponies have been on the islands since the Norsemen arrived but are becoming increasing rare in the wild. They vary in size from thirty-six inches to forty-five inches at the shoulder and they come in all colors from black, dark brown, light gray, chestnut, and combinations thereof. The ponies look their best in the late summer when they have shed the entire winter coat but since it was January any I saw would be at their shaggiest.

As soon as we were on the road in our rental car, I began my hunt for ponies. This was not an easy task as it was pouring down rain mixed with a little sleet. I kept my nose pressed to the window so I would not miss one pony. Frustrated, I had to wipe the moisture from the window every few minutes. For the first thirty minutes I saw nothing but gray, damp Shetland landscape. I began to worry that the reports I had read about how rare it was to see the ponies in the wild were true. As we passed Lerwick on our way north, I began to lose hope.

And then! Just off of my side of the car were three ponies sheltered behind a hillock.

'There they are, off to the right!' I screamed.

Dean, who was driving and, Sue who was navigating, jumped like they had been shot. By the time I explained, it was too late for them to see what I was so excited about. The ponies were out of sight

As we drove into the car-park of the St Magnus Hotel located at the top of St Magnus Bay in northern part of the main Shetland Island, what was in the front garden but three Shetland ponies! I went crazy. I wanted desperately to take their picture but the rain and sleet had not stopped so I went inside without a photograph. As soon as we were in our room I looked out of the window, but the ponies were gone.

While we ate lunch I asked our hostess if ponies were common in the area. She smiled and reassured me there were too many wild ponies in the area as they have a tendency to eat flowers and destroy gardens. She gave me hope that later we would see ponies again. But, we did not see any more that day.

The area around Hillswick is impressive because of the many stacks in the huge bay of St Magnus. Our appointment to meet the key-holder for the lighthouse was two hours away but we could not stand the suspense any longer. Calling the key-keeper we told him we would be at the lighthouse in ten minutes. Nervous and wanting the area to be everything Rob described, we drove the six miles to the lighthouse. In the Shetlands you are almost always surrounded by magnificent views of the sea and the road leading to Eshaness Lighthouse has some of the best. Almost all the way to the lighthouse you can see the spectacular St Magnus Bay with its famous Da Drongs and Dore Holm.

I could see the wee lighthouse with its ocean backdrop as we came up the hill. It was gorgeous. As we got out of the car the first things I saw were the world famous Eshaness cliffs. Pictures cannot do this particular spot justice since so much of its splendor is the sound of the waves and the smell of the ocean. Before we entered the lighthouse accommodation door I knew this was what all the waiting had been for.

Built in 1929 by David A. Stevenson, Eshaness was young, by Scottish lighthouse standards. After all the weather problems I hoped the fact that it was designed by a member of the Stevenson family, known as the world's greatest lighthouse engineers, would convince Dean it was worth considering. It has a unique square white tower, which is only twelve meters high. Dean called it 'squatty'. The station sits on a cliff over two hundred feet above the ocean so it has the elevation necessary to send its beam 25 miles into the sea. The station is small by Scottish lighthouse standards since it had only one keeper. The previous owners had completely renovated the living quarters. Just inside the main door is a beautifully framed picture of the dedication of Eshaness in 1929. The former owner's fondness for Eshaness was evident in every inch of the building. The paintwork had been stripped back to its original wood. We all felt sad that the owner had died and that his widow had had to leave. They must have loved it so. By the time we had walked through the house we knew we would make an offer.

We went back to our hotel, took over a table in the bar, and diagrammed the facility to determine furniture needs. Later that night we talked with the assistant manager of the hotel about services available in the area. The National Health Service surgery was only six miles from the lighthouse. A bus picks you up right at your front door and connects with the major bus lines going to Lerwick or the airport, so you could get around without a car. The more we looked around the more we realized that Eshaness had more positive assets than any lighthouse we had ever considered.

This was it and we all knew it. The problem now was could we buy it.

Thrilled but Scared,
Sharma

Date sent: Wednesday, 13 January 1999
Subject: **The Worst Ferry Ride in History**
To: rampaint@world.net

Ray and Marylou,

A gale set in last night and we got to experience a furious storm on the west coast of Shetland. 'The little man in the black box', as Shetlanders call the BBC weather forecaster, said we would have snow with the winds. Dean and Sue were concerned we would get trapped in Hillswick. Personally I thought it would be fun to spend a couple more days there. It was cozy sleeping in the solid old St Magnus while the winds wailed around the building.

The next morning it was a bright clear day with pale blue skies over the sparkling gray water of St Magnus Bay. Looking out of the window I saw them. Three Shetland ponies were gnawing grass in the front yard of the hotel. I grabbed my camera and ran for the front door. Just before I opened the door I calmed down enough to move slowly so I would not scare them if they were still there. I could see they were no longer in the hotel's yard but had moved across the road to better grass beside the bay. Very slowly I walked closer so I could get a good photo. The lead pony eyed me with distrust so I stopped. He began grazing again and I moved closer. I started taking pictures hoping they would hold still long enough that I would get one good picture. Naturally I ran out of film, so I just stood and

watched these handsome creatures. It was a blessing that I ran
out of film because those few moments alone with the ponies
I will always treasure. I watched while they chewed their grass,
swished their tails, and whinnied to each other as they left.
It was probably only a few minutes before they trotted down the
road, but what moments they were. To be so close to a wild
creature becoming so rare is a gift and I am thankful for the
opportunity.

As soon as Dean and Sue could get me away from the ponies
we left the hotel. We wanted to check out Lerwick, which would
be our BIG city if we were able to buy the lighthouse. The snow
did not come near us even though we could see snow had turned
Ronas Hill white as we drove towards Lerwick. Lerwick is an
interesting town built on hills which go right down to the
harbor. It has many appealing shops. I wished we could have had
more time to spend just looking around. Actually we spent most
of our three hours in Lerwick's furniture stores. If we could pick
out some furniture this trip then we might be able to order and
have it delivered to the lighthouse after we purchase it. (I am
trying to use positive thinking to help us succeed.)

Our plan was to take the P&O ferry to Aberdeen so we could
check out all means of transportation. It's an all night ride leaving at 6:00 pm and arriving the next morning in Aberdeen at
8:00 pm. We rented a private cabin for three. When we got to
the ferry terminal they had posted the weather forecast for gale
force 8 – 9 winds that sounded like a 'little' rough. We were
undecided whether to cancel our reservations and get a plane out
before the winds started or to go on the ferry. After much debate
we chose to stay with the ferry since it was a lot cheaper than
last minute plane reservations.

While we were at the ferry terminal I called our solicitor and
instructed him to submit a bid for Eshaness based on the survey
I had gotten before we left the States. After I called we kept
discussing different offers that would make the bid more appealing. I ended up calling the solicitor again from the ferry with

some more thoughts related to the bid. He convinced us the safest way was to make a clean offer for the property and forget any fancy terms.

I ate dinner early and retired to the cabin. The best place to be on a ferry in a gale is in bed. Dean gets extremely seasick on a regular ride so he decided he would stay up in the lounge where he would not keep us awake as he threw up all night. Sue wasn't sure how she would react but she stayed with him for a while.

I had ridden ferries in gales but nothing that even compared with this. Standing up and walking anywhere was only possible if you were holding on to something, and even then it was difficult. I just settled into my bunk and read my book. Sue finally arrived in the cabin after a thrilling up and down journey from the lounge to the cabin. The rest of the night turned out to be entertaining for Sue and I. Neither of us were seasick but getting around the cabin was hysterical. I will never understand why Sue decided she would have more room in the upper bunk bed. Getting into the upper was a challenge with the boat swaying so hard but getting down in the middle of the night was even worse. I kept warning her if she did get down it would be a supreme trial to reach the bathroom. I had tried twice and ended up crawling on my hands and knees. As she tried desperately to get her foot on the ladder I could not stop laughing. She would almost have her foot on the ladder and the boat would lurch. Then all I could see was one bare foot dangling in the air searching for the ladder. I laughed so hard tears ran down my face.

We didn't see Dean until the next morning. He had had a rough night, which he did not want to talk about. All I could think was how glad I am we made our bid for Eshaness before we left Lerwick or he might have been against it. I was getting more and more worried about him saying 'no' because of all our weather problems.

Later we learned that the next ferry which left Lerwick had to turn back as the sea was so rough. I was really glad we had made the bid before we left.

The Sailor,
Sharma

Date sent: Wednesday, 13 January 1999
Subject: **Snow Comes to Speyside**
To: rampaint@world.net

After arriving in Aberdeen where it felt great to have our feet on ground which did not shake and roll, we headed for the train station. Once seated on the train to Nairn we welcomed the clickety-click of the wheels as they carried us across the beautiful landscape. We were elated it was wheels running on land instead of a ship riding a rugged sea. Since sleep was scarce on the ferry we dozed off and missed the scenery. When we woke we knew Nairn was near as high mountains could be seen in the distance.

Nairn station was the cleanest and neatest train station we had ever seen in Scotland. As we waited on Robert Macdonald to pick us up we all fell asleep again. Finally, Robert arrived and we were on our way to Castle Grant Farm just outside Grantown-on-Spey. Robert was late because the road between Nairn and the farm has been covered with ice.

By this time we were more than a little paranoid about the weather. We had so far been delayed leaving the States by a blizzard, ice-bound in Thurso, encountered snow and sleet in the Shetlands, and experienced a horrendous ferry ride in a gale. Well, you may say this was January what did we expect. Our January trips to Scotland for the last seven years had never been anything like this.

Robert told us the forecast tonight was for snow. (Yikes, it begins again!) He assured us it was only going to be a few inches. Right after dinner we began seeing the biggest fattest snowflakes ever outside the window. Well, here comes our few inches.

By morning the few inches had turned into nine! Sue had to fly from Inverness to London that afternoon so right after breakfast the phone calls began. Inverness airport was closed and the trains were running an hour to two hours behind. If she could get to Glasgow, the airport there was open. It looked like a train to Glasgow was her best bet. One minor problem remained. Could she get from the farm to Aviemore? One option was to take the tractor the fifteen miles to Aviemore but it was obvious that idea did not really appeal to Sue. At about 10:00 am the snow stopped and the sun came out. We decided to wait a couple of hours and then send Robert out in the truck to see what the roads to Aviemore were like.

Well, since we had nothing to do but wait, the Macdonald children, Sarah and Jenny, whom I love dearly, persuaded me a snowman was what we should do. So out we went. It was to be a snowman but with its long straw hair it was definitely more a snow lady.

It came time to test the roads so the brave Macdonald parents were off in the truck to Grantown-on-Spey to buy milk. We wished them well with a few snowballs. The girls and I decided to build a sledge run down a hill behind the house. This was a major undertaking because in addition to making the path we wanted to ice it down so the sledge would go FAST. We had almost finished the sledge run when Robert and Margaret returned and said the roads were partially open. Sue should make leave for Aviemore.

Robert and Sue took off immediately in the truck. I decided I had enough of snow construction and desperately needed a cup of tea. I had not been in the house more than ten minutes when a blizzard hit. I mean a total white out. You could not see our beautiful snow lady only a few feet from the kitchen window. Minutes seemed like hours as the snow continued to fall and Robert was not back. Finally Robert arrived. Sue made the train but the trip back from Aviemore had been treacherous.

It continued to snow until we had over eighteen inches on the ground. The girls were disappointed it was a weekend. They were sure they would have gotten out of school if it had been during the week. Robert and Dean set about feeding the sheep and cows. This was no easy task in eighteen inches of snow with drifts and the snow still coming down. I felt sorry for the sheep

as they huddled into the snow banks. Dean asked me why
I didn't feel sorry for the two men who had to go out and feed
them?

As soon as the snow stopped I was out with my camera taking pictures of the area in its heavy coat of white. Everyone else
was frustrated with the snow but to me it was so incredibly
beautiful and I loved every minute of it.

The Scottish Snow Bird,
Sharma

Date sent: Thursday, 18 February 1999
Subject: **Bid for Eshaness**
To: Susie@world.net

Susie,

We are back in the good old US of A.

It's happened again. Our bid for Eshaness was turned down
flat. The owner's solicitor responded that the bid was too low.
He indicated there was some concern about the accuracy of the
survey we had secured.

As soon as we could we hired another surveyor to look at
the property. His survey came in only £5,000 more than the first
one. We decided to offer £5,000 more than the new value. It was
again rejected. We were so close to our goal but stumped again.
It is hard to believe the owner would not take £5,000 over the
surveyed value. The owner wanted to have a structural survey
done, which she hoped would support her position. Again everything stopped because for some reason the structural survey
wasn't done.

The owner felt the first surveyor's concern about the roof
needing replacing in the near future was keeping the valuation
price low. Suddenly I had a brainstorm. What if we had the two

surveyors indicate in writing what the property would be worth if there were no concerns about the roof. Our solicitor thought it was worth a try so letters were secured and we made an offer £10,000 above the amount indicated in those letters. We are waiting...

Hopeful,
Sharma

Date sent: Thursday, 18 March 1999
Subject: **We Got It**
To: @LIST4E69.PML

This morning very early, Dean came upstairs holding a fax by the corner with a rather strange look on his face. I looked at him and knew our latest offer for Eshaness Lighthouse had been accepted. It had finally happened. I read that fax over and over trying to believe the words. For eight years I had been waiting to see exactly those words on a piece of paper. Now, they were finally in front of me. It was still early in the morning but I couldn't wait. People would just have to wake up. I called the people who had physically been involved in visiting the light-houses including my friend Sue, my brother and his wife. When they answered the phone the simple message was 'We got it'. They immediately knew what I meant and they were as happy as we were. The search was finally over. We had our Scottish light-house home.

There was a great deal of fear along with the joy. I think this experience is called 'Buyer's Remorse'. An offer in Scotland is binding so we were now going to have to use all the money we had been accumulating. The bid had been so high we could buy just a few pieces of furniture at first and my writing must continue to be successful to support the small mortgage. Eshaness seems further away now that it is our responsibility.

We have to find a way to make sure it is well taken care of.
I knew my worries were normal but I kept trying to not think
about them and enjoy the fact after eight years we had finally
succeeded.

I Still Can't Believe It,
Sharma

PART TWO

GETTING READY

Date sent: Thursday, 25 March 1999
Subject: **Paperwork**
To: Susie@world.net

Well, we signed all the papers to close the purchase of Eshaness
Lighthouse. It has gone surprisingly well considering the distance
involved. There does not seem to be as many papers to sign in
Scotland to close a house as in the United States. I have always
been amazed when you go into a house closing in the US that
you must sign twenty papers at least.

Part of what has made it so easy is that Ronnie Cameron at
the Bank of Scotland in Thurso is so thorough. I guess it nice to
know we got one good thing out of all those trips to Thurso; we
met Ronnie. We are going to keep our bank accounts and the
mortgage at the Thurso Bank because of him. I say a prayer of
thanks every time it goes so smoothly.

Derek Rayburn, our solicitor, at Rankin and Aitken has been
a fantastic. He even helped us get our telephone connected at
Eshaness. When the fax came with the telephone number on it
I cried and cried with joy. A UK telephone number had always
been just a fantasy. Now right there in front of me in black and
white was Dean Krauskopf, Eshaness Lighthouse and the
number. Seeing that number made me finally realize that it was
true. We are going to have a home in Scotland.

One big disappointment is that Dean will not be able to
come with me to take possession of Eshaness. I was hoping he
would be able to go but it is the busiest time of year for him. It
is more than a little bit frightening to think I am going to go
over there all by myself to such an isolated place. We bought it
for its isolation but I never thought I would be alone for the first
trip.

We need a good caretaker and someone I could call on in case of emergency when I am alone. Dean and I really liked Tom Williamson, who showed us the property and kept the keys for the current owner. He probably does not live too far from the lighthouse and he certainly seemed reliable and fond of the lighthouse. What do you think?

Trying to Get Everything Organized,
Sharma

Date sent: Monday, 29 March 1999
Subject: **Caretaker**
To: Susie@world.net

Susie,

Thanks for the input on the selection of Tom Williamson as the caretaker for Eshaness. I talked to him on the telephone today and he would be delighted to look after the building for us. I am still having a little trouble understanding the Shetland accent but that will pass with time I am sure.

It is sort of strange how things happen. This search for a lighthouse home started in Stranraer eight years ago. Two people who helped us immensely were Tom Kelly, the attendant at Corsewall, and Tom Mitchell, the banker who helped me with the business plan. Now that the search is over we have another helpful Tom but this time at the other end of Scotland. I wonder if all the Toms in Scotland are so helpful by nature, or have we just been lucky.

My airline ticket arrived and I will be taking possession of Eshaness on 1 May – big moment for all of us. After much hassle I have ordered a bed, kitchen table with chairs and the futon chair we looked at in January in Lerwick. The futon chair I will use to sleep in the room with the Rayburn if the electricity goes out. I wish I could get more furniture but as you know it took the entire lighthouse fund to buy Eshaness so I am going to be quite comfortable with what I have gotten.

Soon To Be Resident of Scotland,
Sharma

Date sent: Tuesday, 30 March 1999
Subject: **The Box**
To: Susie@world.net

Sue,

I have begun to accumulate things to take to the lighthouse. I found out that I could take a box, as long as it's within certain dimensions, as my second piece of luggage without cost. I find myself trying to save as much money as I can. It is quite an undertaking to furnish a house that is over four thousand miles away. You should see the back bedroom. The bed has become a depository for all the 'important' stuff I want to take to Eshaness. It is covered and I have just begun. I keep checking the prices of things in the UK. If the necessary item is available over there for a reasonable price I will get it there; if not I will bring it from the US. First item I bought was a grand set of pots and pans that would have cost a fortune in the UK. I got them for half of the UK price here. I decided to take the cutlery and the dishes I inherited from my Mom. That is not so much a cost cutting factor but a sentimental one.

Dean is concerned that I'll need tools. Since he is not going to be with me to buy the right ones (!) he went out and bought a whole horde of things. Half of them I do not know how to use but if I need them I guess I will have them.

Since there is a difference in the way bath towels and linens are made in the UK; I am taking towels from here. It isn't that the ones over there will not work it is just what we are used to. We are all creatures of habit.

The Packer,
Sharma

Date sent: Thursday, 1 April 1999
Subject: **Pictures**
To: Susie@world.net

Susie,

I have decided that I am going to take pictures of Michigan and our farm to hang at Eshaness. When we have accumulated some good pictures of Eshaness I will hang them here. That way if we get homesick for the one where we are not currently residing we will have reminders of the other. Homesick is not quite accurate since we now have two homes but you get the idea. It is not going to be easy having two homes; both are beautiful and well suited to our values but four thousand miles apart. I know rich people have European homes but Dean and I do not fit into that category. We have to shop for the cheapest airline tickets just to visit the lighthouse.

The first picture I am taking to Eshaness is an original watercolor of a Great Lakes lighthouse we brought at the library's silent auction. I also sent off a package to Tom today with some pictures of Michigan flowers. Deciding what other pictures to take will be difficult as I have so many and only so much room in the box.

Pictures have always been important to me when we moved into a new place. Once the pictures are hung I feel more like the new place is mine.

The Decorator,
Sharma

Date sent: Tuesday, 13 April 1999
Subject   **Crisis – New Box**
To: Susie@world.net

Sue,

I got all of my things packed in the box but I couldn't lift it.
The weight limit is sixty pounds on British Airways for
international luggage and the current box must weigh a hundred
pounds. With much grumbling and irritation I unpacked the box
putting everything back on the bed. Since the new box is smaller
I will have to eliminate some carefully chosen items. Which ones
to eliminate is the problem? After spending so much time
choosing in the first place and now having to leave some of them
behind is exasperating.

Dean says I cannot leave the tools or the battery operated
portable short wave radio. It looks like some of the pictures will
have to stay here since they are bulky. Tom said the ones I sent
via mail had broken glass so I won't send pictures that way
again. Tonight I will try to pack the box without the pictures
and see what happens. If that does not work maybe I will have
to buy expensive 'wellies' over there and leave mine behind.

My airline ticket came today and I looked at it with a sense
of wonder. This is not just another trip to look for a lighthouse.
This time I am going to be living in our own keeper's accommodations. Exciting times if I could just get all of my things into the
blankety-blank box.

Frustrated Packer,
Sharma

Date sent: Tuesday, 27 April 1999
Subject: **One Day until E-Day**
To: Susie@world.net

Sue,

It is only one day until 'E-Day' better known as Eshaness depar-
ture day. Everything has been jammed into the smaller box. The
only things I had to leave out were two pictures.

   Our solicitor called this morning and it seems I signed one of
the papers in two places with different names. In one signature
I included my middle initial and one I did not. The two Scottish
solicitors are in a panic because they are not technically supposed to let me have possession of the house without all the
paperwork being correct. After many phone calls back and forth
they have worked out a way that I can sign again when I pick up
the keys at the solicitors' in Lerwick.

   I am nervous enough without some last minute problem with
the paperwork. As I get closer to getting on the airplane the
more I want Dean to go with me. What if something goes wrong
with the electricity or the hot water tank does not work? All
kinds of things could go wrong but the contractor from Brae
inspected the lighthouse and he said everything was working.
The most comforting fact is that the telephone is on and working. I called our Eshaness number today and it rang. No one
answered of course but at least it works.

A Bundle of Nerves,
Sharma

Date sent: Wednesday, 28 April 1999
Subject: **E-Day**
To: Susie@world.net

E-day is finally here. My suitcase is all packed. The box is on its wheels so I can get it from the car into the airport. Once the airline takes possession of the box I will only need to shift it from the conveyor in Sumburgh, Shetland's airport, to the bus. The list of things to do has been checked a dozen times to see if I left something off but I don't think I did.

Dean will have to meet me at the airport in Detroit instead of taking me to the plane. I rented a car to drive the ninety miles to the airport in Detroit where I will just drop the rental car so I will not have my car in the parking lot for a month.

Robin, my next-door neighbor, took me to get the rental car and came back to the house to help me load the box into the car. (This box is getting to be a pain.)

She had purchased a beautiful pink carnation corsage for me to mark this special occasion. What a nice gesture and I will definitely wear it all the way to the lighthouse. It probably will look a little battered after the all night flight but I am still going to wear it.

I am about to put my e-mail on forwarding and take off for the plane. If the traveling all goes well I'll e-mail you from the B&B in Lerwick before I pick up the keys to the lighthouse and gather the furniture.

To be perfectly honest, I am a nervous wreck and scared to death.

Sort of Ready,
Sharma

PART THREE

THE FIRST TRIP – MAY IN SHETLAND

Date sent: Thursday, 29 April 1999
Subject: **Arrived – Finally**
To: @LIST5E23.PML

Susie,

I am at the B&B but arrived very late. As we know flying is not
an exact science. No problem until I arrived at Aberdeen but
Sumburgh airport was fogged in. The flight before I arrived had
flown all the way up to the Shetlands only to find it was still too
foggy and had to return. After a short delay they called our
flight, which was full with the flight before not making it.
My seatmate was head of the Water Authority in Shetland and
I asked him if flying all the way to Shetland only to have to turn
around and fly back was unusual. Laughing he told me it
happens many times as Sumburgh was in the part of the island
that was prone to fog. We got to the Shetlands without a
problem but once we got near the airport all you could see
below was cloud cover. The pilot tried three approaches but had
to abort at the last minute on each. Reluctantly he announced
we would be flying back to Aberdeen. I was crushed. So close to
getting the lighthouse but now the silly fog would not let me
land. When we arrived back at Aberdeen they asked all of us to
go to the check-in desk. British Airways was offering to take us
to the ferry and pay our ferry fee. Fog would not detain the ferry
and anyone taking this option would be guaranteed to arrive the
next morning. My seatmate seeing how upset I was at the delay
whispered to me that we should stay on the airplane because
usually the last flight of the day made it. Feeling I could trust
him I did not take the ferry option and stayed with the airline.
We had a three-hour delay until the next flight so my new friend
and I decided to have a bite to eat. He was a member of the BA

Club so we went into their private area where they had snacks and drinks. What an interesting experience that turned out to be. The room was packed. Most of the people were London consultants to the oil companies based in Aberdeen. When they called the London flight the room emptied just like magic. I think that was the first time I truly realized how important oil was to the area and how much money was involved.

We sat in the Club and watched the clock. The Aberdeen airport had a 10:00 pm curfew, which meant we had to get out of Aberdeen before 8:00 pm. It takes an hour to fly to Shetland and if we had to turn back again we would not be able to land in Aberdeen after 10:00 pm. Just before 8:00 they called our flight. When we arrived in the general area of Shetland the pilot announced a strong wind had come up and had blown the fog away. Fantastic, we are going to get to land. What the pilot did not mention was that the strong wind would make an extremely bumpy landing. But, land we did and I was finally in Shetland.

On the flight up I worried that the bus would not be operating, as it would be so late when we arrived. My new friend and seatmate volunteered to give me a ride to my B&B from the airport. Never once did it occur to me that it might be dangerous to go with a complete stranger in a car late at night. In the short time I had known him he had been so kind and helpful. The bus was waiting for us when we landed but I still took the luxury of a car ride with someone who would help me with my box. The one thing I have to give British Airways credit for is the box and luggage is here so that part went well.

The Soon-to-be Lighthouse Keeper,
Sharma

Date sent: Friday, 30 April 1999
Subject: **Hectic First Morning in Shetland**
To: @LIST5E23.PML

Greetings from Shetland,

I am on my way to get the keys to our new home on a beautiful sunny day. After I get the keys I have to rush around and purchase odds and ends including a television set. Also I will need to get groceries for the next three days since it will Monday before I can get back in town. I think I told you before I left that the furniture store was going to allow me to ride in the truck with the furniture to the lighthouse. That means I have to be at the furniture place by 1:00 pm so the workers can get back from the lighthouse before evening tea.

I am off to pick up the keys to Eshaness and see how quickly I can shop in a town in which I have only spent two hours.

Hopefully I will survive all of this pressure. I am really nervous. As soon as I can I will e-mail you all.

The New Shetland Resident,
Sharma

Date sent: Friday, 30 April 1999
Subject: **I am the Lighthouse Keeper**
To: @LIST5E23.PML

Hi! All!

I am sitting at the dining room table at Eshaness Lighthouse watching the light beam reflected on the distant hills. It has been a warm and clear day, which made the move a little bit easier. It was a frantic day. I was able to get the television, go to the library and get groceries before I went to the furniture store to ride with the van out to the lighthouse. The ferry was late so the van had just left for the ferry to get my new table. The owner of the furniture store took me to his house for lunch. His home was

in the older part of Lerwick on the hill behind the harbor.
They had remodeled an ancient house and it was beautiful.
Only in the Shetlands would the owner of the town's biggest
furniture store take a customer to his house for lunch with his
family. Not only did I have a great lunch, but also I learned a lot
about Lerwick and where to shop for things. Finally two hours
late with table on board we left in the van for Eshaness. Spring is
just beginning in Shetland. The hills are literally covered with
daffodils except of course where the sheep have had them for
lunch. It is also lambing season and I saw hundreds of lambs
everywhere. They are so cute.

The day was so clear and bright it almost hurt my eyes.
The ocean sparkled in the intense sunlight. The ride from
Lerwick was breathtaking. It was totally different from the two
days in January we made the same drive. The color of the sea
was intense blue with no white swells. I could hardly wait to get
to the lighthouse to see it in sunshine. We had not seen the lighthouse in sunshine during our winter visit.

I had planned a picnic out on the rocks by the ocean to
watch the light in the tower but it took so long to get everything
set up I ate supper after dark.

Tom was here when we arrived. He probably had spent many
hours waiting. I had tried calling both his house and the lighthouse
to tell them we would be late but had no luck reaching him at
either place. The furniture store man was glad Tom was here since
he needed another pair of hands to put the furniture together.

Beautiful coastline and surf can be seen out of almost every
window. As I washed dishes I watched the surf. When I wake up
in the morning there will be surf right outside my bedroom
window. It is a very 'oceanie' place.

The inside of the house is so beautiful you forget this is a
historic building. One frustration is I have to read the
instructions on all the appliances to make them work. The stove
has two different types of ovens and the burners are halogen
under glass. It is a riot trying to figure all of this out.

The appliances are nothing compared to the difficulties with the Rayburn.

To get the Rayburn started I have to clean out all of the ashes then using fire-starters and wood try to get the coal to catch fire. The fire-starters ignite quickly. I burned two fingers already. Learning the right amount of coal to put in the stove so I keep the water hot and this room warm is not easy. So far I have had to run the cold water at least seven times to keep the hot water heater from exploding because the water was boiling. There is no doubt in my mind that I will not be able to keep the Rayburn burning all night. Caretaker Tom is taking me to Brae to get the things I forgot in Lerwick like a knife, pillow, and paper towels. He said he would restart the Rayburn for me if it went out.

Since the windows are closed you cannot hear surf. Three-foot wide walls are great insulators. I am going out in a few minutes to try to take a picture since a beautiful full moon just rose over the hills. It should be reflected in the water. My camera probably won't get anything but it is worth a try. There are million pictures here and it is changing every minute so that makes a million more.

Eshaness is a busy place with sea-birds and the sound of the ocean but it is also deeply still. I know that sounds like a contradiction but what is missing are all the sounds involved with civilization. You hear no cars, people, or even airplanes. When I go outside my only company is the constantly revolving beacon from the tower. It might be scary if it wasn't so calming. Tonight I promised myself to talk to Dean about making a pact that we would not bring the chaos of our life at the farm to the lighthouse. If we were not so far from everything I would have the phone disconnected. The one thing we can do is not give the number out to many people.

I will write tomorrow, as the moon cannot be missed.

The Lighthouse Keeper,
Sharma

Date sent: Saturday, 1 May 1999
Subject: **Second Day as Keeper**
To: @LIST5E23.PML

Hi!

The song 'It's May It's May the Lovely Month of May' keeps going through my head. It is a beautiful Saturday at Eshaness. The sun is dazzling and very warm. Being a Saturday we have twenty-five tourist cars in the car-park. (So much for no noise or signs of civilization at the lighthouse.) The procedure for tourists visiting Eshaness seems to be to drive to the car-park and sit in your car and stare at the cliffs or stand in the car-park and take pictures of our house and the coastline. One lady came up and asked if she could use the rest room. I said no. Once we started that it would never end. Tourists hopefully are only a weekend activity and will not be around much during the week.

Tom and I made our trip to Brae. You will have to see the Brae Building Center to believe it. It isn't a large store but it has almost anything you would get in a huge building center back in the US and the people are so friendly. The problem is you have to know where to look for objects since things are piled on top of each other or hidden back in corners. Tom and I asked the owner if they had any small Rugosa roses so we could plant them in the lighthouse's yard. Of course they did. We had to look out in the open area in front behind some large plants and there they were.

When Tom and I were planting the Rugosa roses a tourist came up and asked if we lived here. I told him I did. He said he thought this was one of the most beautiful coastal spots in the world. I cannot disagree with that statement. It is absolutely gorgeous and in every direction is another stunning view. I went for a short walk after lunch and found a weathered old Celtic stone cross. It was covered with moss and ancient looking. I am taking the weekend off from my writing, as the weather is just too nice. I will get back to writing next week when it is supposed to rain. Or maybe I will just watch it rain. The lighthouse is for peace not work.

During the evening light I will take some more pictures. I keep looking for puffins. They have not arrived but oyster-catchers are everywhere. They are black and white and shimmer in the sun. Their song sounds like a cross between a chirp and quiet honk. The birds are not afraid of me and I can get in close proximity to them. They have no reason to be afraid as few people venture away from the car-park. So far most of the time I have been the only person around, except for today. By dusk even the tourists have left.

Tom is going fishing tomorrow and maybe fresh fish will be on the menu.

The Rugosa roses, or as Tom calls them, 'my trees', are about as close as we can come to a tree that can be raised at the lighthouse. Tom and I planted the four Rugosas. Everyone says they grow very well in the Shetland environment. Eshaness is the not a normal Shetland location so we are experimenting to find a place in the garden where they might survive. The storms from the west can be violent and will destroy everything growing in their path so all the roses have gone on the east side of the house.

The most popular story people tell me is about the storm a few years ago when a five-foot boulder was tossed on the roof of the lighthouse. The lighthouse sits two hundred feet above the sea so it was a pretty violent storm that could throw a boulder so far.

Back to the flowers, I will just have to wait and see how the roses do. When I come back next time, if they are still alive after being unattended maybe we have a chance. I brought primula and heather seeds. I want to plant those around the sundial. I also will put some heather seeds on the sea side where it will be harder to get something to grow.

That's all for now. I am off to sit on a rock in the sun and watch for Orca whales and just enjoy being here. Orcas have been spotted on the east side of the mainland so I have high hopes I will see some before I leave.

The Lighthouse Gardener,
Sharma

Date sent: Saturday, 1 May 1999
Subject: **X-rated Behavior**
To: @LIST5E23.PML

Hi!

I am sitting at the table eating my toast and looking out the window. On top of the garage are two seagulls that are conducting themselves in a most improper manner. It is spring here so all of the wildlife is going about the business of continuing their species. But – do these two gulls have to mate on top of our garage. They seem to have no concern that it is a public place and I might be watching. Even worse since it is Saturday what'll the tourists think of this behavior? The lighthouse has become a brothel for seagulls. Oh, such embarrassment. I think I will stay inside until those birds are through or leave.

The Brothel Keeper,
Sharma

Date sent: Saturday, 1 May 1999
Subject: **Keys and a Treasure Chest**
To: @LIST5E23.PML

Greetings,

Tom and I were out in the tool rooms trying to find the locks that matched the keys. When I picked up the keys from the solicitor they handed me a big padded envelope full of keys.

There are more locks here than you would find in a bank and it is frustrating trying to figure out which key fits where. Tom thinks it is ridiculous. Most people here do not even keep their doors locked. Another funny thing is that there is a surveillance camera on the water tank. What we haven't figured out is where the picture goes. I guess we'll have to ask Leslie. (Leslie Johnson is the light's attendant and Tom's half-brother).

Rummaging around in the workshop we found the last owner had left most of her husband's tools. Dean will be thrilled. When we were here in January we only gave the generator house that has been converted to workshops and an office a quick glance. Since I am not technically inclined I have no idea what half of the stuff is. The former owner's husband was an electrical engineer so there is some very complex equipment and sturdy army boxes to store things in. Dean will love it since tools are a passion of his.

The little TV I bought is doing real well now it is hooked up to the aerial on the tower. When the weather gets bad it sometimes fades into snow but most of the time it is sharp. Tom keeps me informed on what is worth seeing by giving me a ring when something good is on. One of Tom's favorite activities is watching TV. I also found a web page that gives the evening schedule so I take notes of anything I want to watch. I especially look for those great comedies and murder series that are broadcast in the States after they are over in the UK. We gave up watching TV back in the States but here it is part of learning about the culture.

Eshaness may be isolated but every morning when I turn on my computer to get the weather and my e-mail I can find out just about anything I want to know. Best of all worlds is to get information only if you need it. The problem with Internet access here is you have to pay for every minute you are online. The charge is not from the Internet Service Provider but the telephone company. Going on-line whenever I want for as long as I want is going to be a hard habit to break. Here I try to go on after 6:00 pm when the rates go down and before 8:00 am in the morning when they go up. At least I have an ISP that uses a 0845 number, which means you dial long distance but only get charged local rates. Don't ask me how it works, I have no idea. One thing for sure, if I was here full time I would have to get more organized in the development and upload of Scottish Radiance.

Col James installed this fantastic weather station on the roof with the dials in my office. I am sure it is wonderful only the question is how does it work! With a lot of struggle I was able to get it hooked up but it's only giving temperature and wind direction not speed or barometric pressure.

Still having trouble with the Rayburn so Tom drops in twice a day to see how it is doing. Do you remember when I told you one of my thrills was that the lighthouse had a Rayburn? Well, I feel differently about that stove now. Maybe it has a grudge against Americans or something. I spent many years as a Girl Scout and taught fire building so why can't I make this STOVE work.

Technically Challenged,
Sharma

Date sent: Saturday, 1 May 1999
Subject: **The Keeper of the Haunted Lighthouse**
To: @LIST5E23.PML

Hello,

This is only my fourth e-mail today. You would think something exciting was going on over here. Dean called today and it was nice to hear his voice instead of using flat old e-mail communication. I think I might be lonely if I did not have the computer to stay in touch. The mix of the isolation of the lighthouse with the ability to stay in touch using modern technology when and if I want is a perfect arrangement.

It is evening and our light is doing its thing. When it sweeps by the window it looks a like a ghost playing around the windows. What a great idea for a children's story! I will definitely write one about a lighthouse ghost one day. There must be a hundreds of stories here just waiting to be written.

The halogen burners on the stove work well, except I got carried away talking to Dean and burned my porridge. Learning to use them will get easier with practice. Speaking of practice, I am cooking a chicken in the Rayburn tonight. This should be interesting. It smells really good.

Dean said our credit card company called and wondered what the large charge was on our credit card. They said it was from some island. It was good service on their part but I was disappointed they did not know where or what the Shetland Islands were.

The Keeper of the Haunted Lighthouse,
Sharma

Date sent: Sunday, 2 May 1999
Subject: **First Sunday Morning**
To: @LIST5E23.PML

Greetings All,

I'm sitting at the kitchen table in the sun, drinking tea and staring at the ocean listening to Mozart playing on my little Grundig Short Wave Radio. The radio is no bigger than the palm of my hand but gets stations all over the world. Dean insisted I get a battery operated short wave radio for emergencies. I am finding it's just plain fun to have around. It is amazing how many stations I can get on this little radio. Most of the time I don't understand the language but there really is a big selection of music. I found three US radio stations so far so Dean will be able to keep track of sports back home. The reception is so good I am going add to my list for later a good short wave radio with better speakers. Music is a big part of my life and somehow it fits with this cozy little house.

I want to share two wonderful moments from last night. First I went out with the camera at sunset to see what pictures I could get. I walked south of the lighthouse because I had not been down that way. There was not a soul around and I could hear the birds and waves from every direction. It was one of the most peaceful moments of my life. I came back and sat on a rock to get a picture of the sunset behind the lighthouse. Two stunning black and white oystercatchers walked up within a foot of me. They are the most exquisite birds. As I mentioned before, they have a strange song. I sat there for over half an hour just watching the sunset with the birds and the incredible gentle sound of the waves for company. Hopefully I got some good pictures.

I could see the moon reflected in the ocean from my bed. It was awesome. The most interesting thing is every once in a while the beacon would go by and change the color of what I could see. You do not want to go to sleep here because you might miss something.

A seagull is sitting on the garage looking at me. I wonder what he wants. We do not have any begging gulls, as that happens because people feed them. Someone told me the Jameses had a pet sea gull but so far I have not seen it.

Report on the ongoing battle with the Rayburn: it did not go out last night for the first time so I had heat in the main room this morning. In fact I had hot water in my new kettle for coffee. Better than a microwave. Also, the chicken I roasted last night came out tender, juicy and brown. I think maybe I will eventually like this Rayburn. It just is taking some getting use to.

I was going to start work on the revision of my novel this morning but it is so beautiful I am going to the broch (prehistoric fort) that is on an island in the Loch of Houlland just a short walk from here. Then I will do my writing. We are supposed to have three more days of clear weather so I want to make the most of it.

The novel revision is important to me but it difficult to stay in the house and write when there is so much to see and do outside. I can't imagine ever being bored here. But, as you all know I don't seem to be bored anywhere. There are just so many neat things to do from reading books to looking at the stars or just watching sky.

The Lighthouse Keeper,
Sharma

Date sent: Sunday, 2 May 1999
Subject: **Sunday Morning Note to Dean**
To: mistysteak@world.net

Dean,

Didn't want to put this in the general e-mail. I have just had a great idea. Please keep my missives from Eshaness, as they would be helpful for my writing. If you keep them on the big computer at home then I will have easy access to them. I still have not figured out how to keep them using world.net's flash mail.

Stupid seagull is still sitting on the garage staring at me. Maybe that is the Jameses' pet after all. I know you are going to say, 'Don't feed it'. It is a fine-looking healthy specimen with a white head and a fat round gray body.

You wanted me to look for cows since we did not see any in January. The cows are kept in the steading during the winter here. The neighbor down the hill by the junction where the Stenness road turns toward the bay keeps cows. Maybe if you talked to him he would agree to board a Belted Galloway and you could have your 'belties' on both sides of the Atlantic.

I know you think Tom will be glad when I leave since he has had to work so hard helping with the flowers and the naughty

Rayburn. Tom is a truly kind person. Besides, he is teaching me so much about Shetland I could not do without his visits.

It was fun hearing about your tree-planting project and I am sorry you sunburned the top of your head. Maybe it would be smart if you wore a hat next time since the hair is getting a little thin on top (Sorry!). I do miss you, the cows, chickens, and Kiri, the wonderful singing dog. It hurts when I think too much about the farm so I guess the best philosophy is not to think about it. In all of my long trips away from home I have always tried not to think about the farm and focus on where I am. I do not allow myself to think a lot about home until the day I get on the plane to come home and it seems to work. I will try to get your radio program on the computer. It is too expensive to listen to all of it because they charge for every minute you are on-line here. A two-hour telephone call even at local rates would be pricey but I will try to listen to some of your program.

One thing I appreciate more and more every day is that buying Eshaness was worth all the pain and agony we went through to get it.

Wifey

Date sent: Monday, 3 May 1999
Subject: **Nearest Neighbors**
To: @LIST5E23.PML

Greetings,

When I first heard that Shetland is one of the sunniest places in Scotland I thought that was just public relations. But, it is another beautiful sunny day at the lighthouse. I am going to spend all day working on my novel but I will be sure to get a few walks in.

My walk to the broch yesterday was worthy of note not because of the broch but how I reacted to the walk itself. I never saw the broch close up. It looks a lot closer than it really is.

I had been walking for about twenty minutes focusing on the broch and watching my footing. The ground is quite smooth but you have to watch the dark green spots in the grass, which means the ground is waterlogged and you could get your shoes soaked. (Without thinking I took off in my regular shoes instead of boots.) Also you have to be on the lookout for holes or rocks that you can stumble over. Stopping to see if there were any picture opportunities, I looked around. It was amazed I could not see the lighthouse nor could I see the sea. Silly as it sounds I became frightened. It was like I had been transported to another world in which I was held prisoner by massive green hills. The broch was in front of me but nothing else was familiar. Having one of those conversations I sometimes have with myself, I said the ocean had to be off to the west and the lighthouse could be easily found by following the cliff above the ocean, but for some reason I could not get up the courage to go on. I hastily turned back and walked as fast as I could until the lighthouse tower was in the distance. Next time I will take a map so I know where everything is located. I have been extremely careful in the hills since if something happens I am a long way from anything and alone.

I discovered our nearest neighbors this morning. Down the hill to the south there are places you can get down to the sea easily by climbing over rocks. Straight out are three little islands inhabited by gray seals. Among the seals are white little fluffs. After I got the binoculars out I could see the white spots were baby seals. I have no way of knowing but I would guess they are probably not a month old. They are ADORABLE. I tried to take a picture of them with my camera but I need a more powerful zoom to see them well. The photos will probably come out as just white spots on rocks. I am going into Lerwick for supplies and groceries tomorrow and will drop my film off. I have been at Eshaness two-and-a-half-days and taken three rolls of film. It will be great to see the pictures.

I also saw a sea pink opening up so I would guess by midweek the hills around here will be a blaze of bright pink. I should get a really good camera before my next trip. The guillemots have arrived. You can see them out on the rocks with their black backs and white breasts. They look a lot like penguins except they have long narrow pointed heads. They are large sea-birds and very graceful. No puffins yet but I hope they are next.

Tom was just here to lend a hand getting the Rayburn going again. That stove is a real pain because it has to be tended all the time. Most everyone around here has converted their Rayburn cookers to burning oil simply because it is easier. I like the coal and am ordering peat tomorrow because I love the smell. The peat is easier to start so it might help. Maybe after a while I will get so I know how much coal to put in at night so I still have coals in the morning. With it going out every night I begin each day with the messy job of restarting it. The former owners left us coal but no wood to use as kindling. There is some wood in the generator house but you need an axe to break it up and Tom is afraid for me to try to do it. Rightly so, I would probably chop my leg off.

Tom is checking his lobster traps and fishing this morning after he checks his lambs. Since it is the middle of lambing season he is quite busy. He has sheep near the lighthouse so he does not have to go out of his way to check on me. I would love to have a lobster but I do not have a pan big enough to cook one. I will either have to buy a pan or wait until next trip. One of the neighbors is bringing me fresh fish for dinner tonight.

It is really tough living in the Shetlands at a lighthouse with so much to do. I need to get started on my revision of the novel but the outdoors are constantly beckoning.

The Seals' New Neighbor,
Sharma

Date sent: Tuesday, 4 May 1999
Subject: **Big Adventure**
To: @LIST5E23.PML

Greetings,

This is the first day I will go to the big (?) city by bus. Being able
to get around without a car is one of the biggest assets of living
here. We cannot afford to buy a car right now. Even if we could
it would be silly to have one that just sits in the garage ninety
per cent of the time. Rental cars are available if we need to make
any trips which cannot be done by bus. Our friends cannot
understand how we can live in this remote area without a car.
I think it is because most Americans are totally dependent on a
car. If we had a car I think we would have a tendency to turn
living here into more like living on the farm by running errands
when we need something. Instead, here we just have to plan
ahead.

The bus can come to the lighthouse twice a day, every day
except Sunday. The 7:10 am minibus takes you to Brae to meet
the big bus to Lerwick. (I won't be using that one very often.
That is earlier than I usually get out of bed.) Its main function is
to get people into Lerwick for work. The minibus at 9:50 in the
morning takes you to Hillswick where you meet the big bus to
Lerwick. For both minibuses I have to call the driver the evening
before, as they do not come all the way to the lighthouse on a
regular run. Bertie, the driver of the 9:50 bus, will I am sure
become a good friend as I will be using that bus a lot since I do
not have a car. The return bus is at 5:10 pm, which gives me
about six hours in Lerwick. That is a lot of time to kill so to
speak. The library is where I will spend most of my time just like
I do in Michigan. There are always new books and CDs to be
checked out. An exciting part of the Lerwick library is their
excellent Shetland collection, which I can use for research.
The mobile library will come to the lighthouse once a month but
since I go into Lerwick so often I probably will not use that as

much. This trip I need to pick up a bird book as the naturalist book I got my first trip to the library had lots of information but not many bird pictures.

The major reason for this trip is to find a place to do my laundry. As always I have a list for more groceries. Starting from bare cupboards with no food or staples there are lots of items I need. Another thing I am learning is when you are so far away from civilization you must keep a detailed list of what you need so that you do not forget anything when you are in town.

No walk this morning so nothing to report on that front. Our good weather is starting to break down. Fronts move so fast around here it is hard to tell what the weather will be from minute to minute. Today is forecast is for sunny and warm changing to rain early this afternoon. The winds seem to increase at night and die down in the day.

I just hope it does not rain before I get back from town. I have put an umbrella in my little cart. One of the necessities I brought in my box is a shopping cart that folds up into a purse-size carrying case. When it unfolds it has sufficient space for bringing things back on the bus.

My one adventure last night was an attempt at taking pictures of the beacon after sunset. I have no idea whether I got any good pictures but I had a good time taking them. First thing when I get into Lerwick I will have my film developed. An even bigger photographic challenge will be trying to catch the tower when it turns on.

There were about ten tourists in the car-park yesterday as it was a Bank Holiday. Two of the cars must have belonged to hikers as the cars were there most of the day. I would expect no more tourists until the weekend now. If we wanted to rent this place during the summer it would be full all the time and is something that might be worth considering.

The Keeper,
Sharma

Date sent: Wednesday, 5 May 1999
Subject: **The Bunker Finally!**
To: @LIST5E23.PML

Hi! There!

My trip to town was an experience. The bus trip was fantastic. No problem with the connections and I met lots of neighbors and friendly people on the buses. Everyone wanted to give me advice since they had heard a lot about 'that nice American that lives at the lighthouse'. How they know I am nice I am not sure but at least the local gossip doesn't call me the grumpy old lady or something similar.

I can't help but be impressed by the bus system. It is a phenomenon. The district council has bought a fleet of minivans, all of which are new and very clean. They are used in the more remote areas first to take children to school and then they pick up people to meet the big bus to go to Lerwick. The big bus is also new and very roomy. An easy access luggage area and no steps means I don't even have to lift my little cart. All of this is paid for or at least supported by money from a multi-million trust fund the council negotiated from the oil companies in exchange for building Europe's largest oil terminal. Everything is paid for by the interest from the trust so the trust remains in case something happens and the oil companies leave. It's not often I would say politicians made good decisions but this certainly was one. Also not often would I say thank you to the oil companies. All the minibus service is free, paid for by council tax and the big bus is only 1 pound 10 pence. When I turn sixty it will be 20 pence. By any definition you would say this is quite a bargain and very convenient.

Learning how to get around in Lerwick is a little difficult. When I asked directions I often got conflicting answers from different people. Needless to say, I did a lot of walking. One trick in Lerwick is to plan your walking so you only have to climb the hill from the harbor to the library once. It's a tough climb. I needed to go from the library to the Co-op to buy groceries so I asked the librarian to call a taxi. I was about walked out. A lady standing by the desk overheard and volunteered to take me to the grocery store. She dropped me off right at the front door. Shetland people are friendly and helpful.

The strangest thing happened. I needed to do some laundry since I did not bring a lot of clothes with me this trip. A small suitcase was all I could handle with the big box. One of the first places I asked directions to was a laundromat or a coin operated laundry. Everyone I asked was puzzled by my question. Finally the librarian told me there were no automatic laundries in Lerwick but there was a laundry where they would do the wash for me quickly. The people at the laundry were extremely accommodating and said they could have my laundry ready before I had to leave on the bus. When I picked the laundry up later in the day I was shocked to find my one small pillowcase of laundry cost £10 to have done. That is almost $17 for one load of laundry. The first thing I am going to buy for the lighthouse when I start buying furnishings is an automatic washer.

The weather is still unbelievable with another sunny day at the lighthouse. I keep thinking it will start raining but there is no major change in the long-range forecast. This morning's walk (I have been walking morning and evening since that is the best light for my photographs) was to a WWII bunker that is on the highest point around here. It lies just south of the Loch of Framgord right behind the lighthouse. I bought a book with Northmavine (the area around me) walks when I was in town. According to the book some of the best views of Eshaness are from the bunker. It is a steep climb. I made it half-way up a couple of times before, but never to the top. Today I finally made it to the top. The bunker fascinated me. I wondered what it was like during the war when the lighthouse was painted gray and the light turned off? Wartime at a lighthouse would make a good setting for a story. Like most Americans, I have never experienced war close at hand and found just standing in the bunker an emotional experience.

You can see miles in every direction from the bunker. It is the only place I have found so far where you can see the lighthouse and Dore Holm, the sea stack, at the same time. I also saw a red bunting bird in the grass on the way there. It has a white moustache. An interesting bird and one I had never seen before. Shetland has many unusual birds.

Great excitement, I saw one pair of puffins. According to a bird book I got at the library the puffins should have arrived or will arrive any day. First they will float near the shore, then they take to the high cliffs to raise their families. I saw my first pair just offshore near the large sea cliff right next to the lighthouse. I hope they nest in the cliff right next door as then I could see them every day.

Believe it or not I had a knock at my door and there stood a nice lady with a beautiful formal flower arrangement in a wicker basket. The bank that helped us buy the lighthouse sent me a basket of spring flowers and the florist had come all the way from Lerwick to deliver them. The driver of the delivery van was looking down the blowhole in front of the lighthouse. Even the local people seem to think a trip to Eshaness is a treat.

First injury at the lighthouse happened last night. I cut my finger trying to open a package. I was frightened. I could not stop it bleeding. Blood was squirting out of my finger. For a few moments I felt I was going to have to call Tom to take me to the doctor or have the doctor come out. It finally did stop bleeding after what seemed to me like hours but was probably minutes. I need an extensive first aid kit here and quickly added that to my list. Also, one should be more careful with knives especially when you are three miles from your nearest neighbors and have no car. I was worried I would not be able to type to work on the novel. But as you can see, typing is not a problem.

The Injured Lighthouse Keeper

Date sent: Wednesday, 5 May 1999
Subject: **Thought You'd Like to Know**
To: mistysteak@world.net

Dean,

After the scare with the cut finger I called the doctor at the surgery in Hillswick to discuss my allergy to bees. Since there is such a short time between the sting and when my breathing could be affected I felt it would be prudent to discuss this with her. The surgery now has my problem on record and will keep in stock the medication that I need if I get stung. I always carry my Epipen to give myself a shot immediately upon being stung, and the necessary follow-up service is only minutes away. I do not think that will be a problem this trip. Since it only gets up into the sixties during the day and drops to the forties at night and I walk in the early morning and after supper the bees and I are not likely to meet. In fact I wonder if we have any kind of stinging creatures out here since the wind is so strong.

Please start thinking about coming here in September. There is so much for you to see and do. Things you might not be able to do in January when the weather is supposed to be so violent. You would get a chance to fish and climb the rocks. In the winter we would just sit inside and listen to the storms, which has its appeal but not for the first trip.

Tomorrow Tom and I are going to the St Magnus and to Brae. He has to get some bands for the lobster's claws. They can cut you dreadfully so they have to have their claws clamped shut. I want to get a lobster kettle. I cannot leave here without eating a lobster if Tom can spare one.

Wifey

Date sent: Thursday, 6 May 1999
Subject: **Return to the St Magnus!**
To: @LIST5E23.PML

Hi!

I am going to walk the cliff down to Moo Stack as soon as
I have cleaned the ashes out of the Rayburn and restarted it.
Moo Stack is the biggest sea stack in pictures of Eshaness cliffs.
You will find a great picture of Moo Stack on my website. It is
another clear sunny day in Shetland and the temperature is very
warm for this time of year. It should reach seventy today. It is
windier than any day so far. I have heard so many stories about
how windy Eshaness is but this is the first day it really has lived
up to its reputation.

Today's planned adventure is to have lunch at the St Magnus
hotel. I wanted to stop by and say 'Hi' to the assistant manager
who was so helpful when we stayed at the hotel in January.
The manager was in England in January when we visited so it
would be nice to meet her too. I may just pop over and meet the
doctor in person since the surgery is right across from the hotel.
Hopefully the Shetland ponies will be around. We have none up
by the lighthouse.

After the St Magnus, Tom is taking me into Brae to get a
lobster pot. I told him I could wait until next trip to have lobster
but he is catching lots of lobsters so he wants me to have one
before I leave. I have never had a lobster caught a few hours
before eating. It ought to be great.

The Hungry Lighthouse Keeper

Date sent: Friday, 7 May 1999
Subject: **Arrivals**
To: @LIST5E23.PML

Greetings

Wouldn't you be surprised to have me write that it is a terrible rainy day at the lighthouse? Well, not this time; we have another great day at Eshaness. I am about to take off for a long walk and want to make sure the Rayburn is burning brightly before I leave. I have been letting it go out early every night since there is no need to heat an empty room. The problem is, I have to wait on it to get started in the morning before I go out. Tom (bless his heart) went to the beach and got me a big bag of drift-wood to use to start it. Using wood to ignite the coal really makes it a whole lot easier.

More birds are arriving every day. Yesterday I saw my first lapwing, which has a long spiked crest on its head; a shag, or as they are called here, a scarf with a funny black feather crown; and a whimbrel that has a long curved bill. Shetland has so many different types of birds and most of them are rare. The birds living around here have their own sanctuary since no one bothers them. They must be on guard for the natural predators of course. The gulls kill baby puffins, which seems so cruel, but that is the way of nature. The puffin population is decreasing but I think it is more because the humans have messed up their natural environment than being killed off by gulls.

I visited the tower last evening. The attendant, Leslie Johnston, was here to do maintenance and he let me see the inside of the tower. There are not many steps to the lantern room so it was fun. One of our disappointments in Eshaness is that it does not have a Fresnel lens. The light source looks like a bunch of headlights put together into a rectangular box. It is large and bulky so the lantern room is crowded. The inside of the tower has ceramic tiles on the walls. The house and the tower both have three-foot thick concrete walls but only the tower has been decorated by tiling it. It just shows the tower is more important in the scheme of things than the house.

I am off to see if I can see the eider ducks in West Loch near Stenness. When we went by the loch in the bus I thought I saw something black and white which just might be a male.

Oh, for the fishermen reading this. In Loch Framgord where the lighthouse had its windmill and we actually still own a few feet of ground they caught an 8-pound brown trout a couple of years ago. This area is supposed to the best loch fishing in Shetland. Leslie, the attendant, is on holiday for two weeks just to fish the lochs. Season is good from May to October so he says.

The Keeper of the Light and the Bird Sanctuary,
Sharma

Date sent: Friday, 7 May 1999
Subject: **Picnic**
To: @LIST5E23.PML

Greetings,

It's me again. I just got back from having a picnic lunch on the rocks in front of the lighthouse. It is so warm and sunny I almost fell asleep. On Shetland you have to be careful in the sun because you can burn easily. Falling asleep in the sun is definitely a no-no. Today would take grand champion for Shetland days. It is about sevnty degrees Fahrenheit with a breeze. The sky has a few puffy clouds but nothing significant. The sea is periwinkle blue so the waves stand out in shocking contrast. Fishing is in full swing. I saw three or four fishing boats go by. They are all small so they stay close to shore and are easy to see. The boats were all different colors and they really stood out against the mirror-like water. I even saw one of the 'wee' Viking boats that some of the fisherman still use. They have been in use since the time of the Viking occupation. Distinct in shape they look a lot like a rowboat but are more square and always painted bright colors.

I planted primula and heather seeds on the sea side of the lighthouse. I have no idea whether they will grow. Both plants are in abundance on Shetland but whether they will grow at windy Eshaness is another story, especially where they are not protected from the west wind.

Speaking of stories I should get back to my novel. As I type on the table my eyes stray to the view outside the window. Seeing the sea makes me want to go out and fool around. I take a break about every two hours and outside I go, usually with cup of tea in hand. My plan has always been that the lighthouse would be my writing retreat, but I'm not sure how productive a retreat it is, as I seem to enjoy being outside too much. A little rain would be helpful in getting the novel rewrite done.

My evening walk will be to see the baby seals. It is only a short distance and maybe they will be more active in the evening. In the morning all they do is lay on the rocks in sun.

If you want to smell something wonderful you should be here to sniff the clothes I dried on the ocean side of the house. I now know why the line is on that side. A clothes soap company could make a fortune if they could patent this smell. It is fresh with a sort of salty touch. The aroma is absolutely divine. It makes the fact that I have to wash clothes by hand without a laundromat in Lerwick not such a hardship. I was worried about my things ending up in the sea if the wind came up but they have special clothespins called 'storm pegs', which keep the clothes on the line even in stiff gales.

The Laundress,
Sharma

Date sent: Saturday, May 8, 1999
Subject: **Second Saturday in Shetland**
To: @LIST5E23.PML

Greetings,

I cannot believe a week has gone by. It is definitely Saturday.
How do I know? The car-park is full of cars. In fact, it might be
a record number since my arrival. It is another picturesque day
but rain is expected before the day is over. Scattered showers
are what they are forecasting. It is surprising that the most
complete and accurate Shetland weather forecast is on
weatherunderground.com, located in Michigan of all places. Not
in my wildest imaginings would I think I would be getting accurate Shetland weather from Michigan.

I seem to be ranging farther and farther on my walks.
This morning I went to the broch, which was the trip that
frightened me that first day. This broch is not as well preserved
as Mousa Broch but it is obvious it was a broch. Brochs are
fascinating as they were places of safety for man and beast.
I must make a trip to Mousa some day and see the world's best-
preserved broch. Our Houlland Broch was located on a small
island to make defending it easier. After visiting the broch I went
half way to the end of the Eshaness peninsula following the cliffs
to the north. Even though I am beginning to know the short cuts
and place markers, I am frightened of the cliffs and will not go
near the edge. I worry about the tourists when they walk right
on the cliff's edge. I suppose that is the best view but I think
staying back is safer.

With more birds arriving every day soon the bird population
will surpass the sheep and people. Being in such a hurry to get
outside I often forget to take my bird book with me so I never
know exactly what I am seeing. This morning I saw what looked
like big flocks of geese flying south. The size of our Canadian
geese and flying in a V, they reminded of the geese in Michigan
but were pure white instead of gray.

I keep looking in the lochs for the fish everyone talks about. They must not hang out near the shore as I have yet to see one. Tom has not caught anything but lobsters so I am waiting for my first fish. I was not keen to try and bring some home on the bus from Lerwick as I have no way to refrigerate them on the way. A local fish van is in this area on Tuesdays and Tom is going to ask her to come to the lighthouse so I will have fish for sure that day. The big question is, what kind to have? There are many different types from those available in Michigan.

I am going to work on the novel only for a short time and then goof off by reading a book on the rocks in the sun over looking the sea. I finally got a mirror and my face is sunburned. I never thought I would need sun block in Shetland but my nose is evidence to the contrary. Shetland is one of the sunniest places in Scotland. Mainland Scotland has had lots of rain since I arrived. Shetland has seen none. The sun is powerful here at this time of year and the days are long. Sunrise is about 5:00 am and sunset is after 9:30 pm. Of course the days will get longer. In June the sun will hardly set and people can go out at 2:00 am and read their newspapers by the gloaming. Gloaming is that in-between light between sunset and dark. I hope in the near future I will be here to read my newspaper at 2:00 am.

Everyone is into gardening right now. Tom is planting his potatoes, which are an important part of his diet. The *Shetland Times* is full of articles about what should be done in gardens. I hope the roses Tom and I planted grow. I have seen marsh marigolds in bloom down by the lochs and a couple of blue violets the sheep missed. Many of the houses are getting trees to grow and there is a forest in the center of the island. I doubt if we will ever have trees out here. But I should never say never and just keep trying.

Speaking of the *Shetland Times*, it is amazing how important that paper is to everyone here. Tom goes to Hillswick first thing every Friday morning to pick it up. I am finding myself becoming addicted to it also. Everything you want to know about Shetland is in there. Right now I am interested in everything so I read every article. I have called a couple of used furniture advertisements but find even by Saturday morning the furniture is sold. I guess if you want used furniture here you must move fast.

The Shetland Times Reader,
The Keeper

Date sent: Saturday, 8 May, 1999
Subject: **Bills**
To: mistysteak@world.net

Dean,

Bills seem to find you wherever you are. I got the solicitor's bill for handling the purchase of Eshaness today as well as the bill for installing the telephone. Would it be possible for me to use the ATM, or cash point as they are called here, for five hundred dollars to pay the solicitor and phone bill? It still is a shock when I convert pounds into dollars. It makes things seem exorbitantly expensive here. Actually I think utilities are more expensive than at home and of course there is always VAT which we get back on goods but not on services. Hopefully I will get used to thinking in pounds not dollars. It just makes me feel worse by converting the cost of everything to dollars. Dollars or pounds, it really costs more to live in the UK.

   The check for the guidebook from my publisher is due any day but naturally it is not here yet. I do not want to be late with my first bill payments.

   I may be half way around the world but one part of life is the same – paying bills and waiting on checks.

   E-mail me today or as soon as you can.

Wifey

Date sent: Sunday, 9 May 1999
Subject: **Blackies**
To: @LIST5E23.PML

Hi!

Some new residents arrived last night. There are hundreds of
black birds chirping in the hills around me. They are called
'Blackies' here and they are very different from our black birds.
They are short and fat for one thing. Their bodies are completely
black except they have a bright yellow bill and longer legs and
their song is not anything like the black birds of the USA. Maybe
I should not be comparing everything to the USA but it is the
only form of reference I have. Shetland is definitely an unusual
place.

It's a little bit cloudy here today. The sun is peeking through
right now so I will be able to take a walk. I am going to Stenness
to stroll on its sandy beach as soon as the Rayburn has a nice
bed of coals. (Yes, I know it seems the Rayburn dictates activities
around here.) Tom found all kinds of driftwood for the Rayburn
on Stenness beach so I might find some other treasures like
shells. I had better put a bag in my pocket in case there is any
new driftwood.

Tomorrow I go into Lerwick to pay bills and shop for
furniture. That way next fall when I go to buy furniture I will
have some point of reference. What I have is fine for one person.
The living room is such a nice room it needs some furniture to
match the beautiful fireplace that is not being used. Definitely, a
washing machine is at the top of the list. If the guidebook check
were to arrive I would buy a washer tomorrow. Then I could
wash up all the sheets and things before I leave.

I seem to have caught a cold but nothing big. My nose is
running and I have a slight sore throat on one side. If it gets any
worse I'll just go to bed and get better. It is a pleasure to be in a

place where absolutely nothing will bother you if you are not feeling well.

Off to Stenness to gather the treasures the sea has left for me.

The Beach Comber,
Sharma

Date sent: Sunday, 9 May 1999
Subject: **A Scottish Mother's Day**
To: @LIST5E23.PML

Hello,

First, I want to wish 'Happy United States Mother's Day' to all of the mothers who are reading this. I am giving myself a happy one by only working on the novel this morning. This afternoon I am taking a book and sitting on my book-reading rock. I have two rocks now. The book-reading rock is flatter and very comfortable while the whalewatching-rock isn't as comfortable but I can see in all directions except east where the lighthouse blocks the view. After rock sitting I am going to listen to Dean on the Internet. He is on from 10 am– 12 pm Eastern USA time, which means he doesn't come on here until 3 pm. For those of you who can't get WJR by radio you can listen to Dean with RealAudio on WJR's website. Sorry I do not have the URL but search for WJR or Radio Detroit.

Getting back from my walk to Stenness beach was a little difficult. I decided to take the road, which is easier because you can look around as you wander. If you go by the hills it is shorter but you must always watch where you are stepping. I suppose when I get to know the hills better I will take the faster route. The road is the definitely the long way to Stenness. It was a delightful walk as the marsh marigolds were blooming along the lochs and burns (streams). I also found huge bunches of wild irises coming up along the burns. I do not know when they bloom but it will be spectacular.

I never noticed before but there is a wee church ruin in the middle of the cemetery down the hill behind the loch. I will put that on my list for tomorrow's walk. I shot another whole roll of film this morning. It is really nice that there is a place in Lerwick where I can get my pictures developed in an hour. Even nicer, it does not cost any more than regular development.

The sand was black at Stenness. I was not surprised because the sand on the Isle of Skye was black. In the south part of the island there is a white sandy beach so I was not sure what to expect. I found some shells. Some? Actually, I found more than I could carry so I left most of them.

Tom has warned me it would be time for the artic terns and I saw my first ones this morning. They are small but stunning with black heads and white and black wings. I found them intimidating. They swoop down like they were going to attack me. They didn't but I felt like they were checking me out for their next meal's entrée. Tom warned me that while the babies are young the adults can fly at you to scare you away. He has even been pecked on his head by a tern that drew blood. There are no terns around the lighthouse as they like to be near the jetties and fishing activities. No fishing at the lighthouse since the sea is two hundred feet below. It would take a long line to catch a fish from Eshaness.

It has been a quiet day. Only a few cars were in the car-park. After two weekends I am an expert on Eshaness tourism and have proof that the majority of the people just sit in the car-park and look at the cliffs. It is considered as one of the most beautiful places in Shetland and on a nice day very peaceful. The folk festival in Lerwick was the reason there were so many tourists last weekend.

I wish I could be here when the tall ships visit in August. It will be such a spectacular sight with some of the largest sailing vessels in the world sailing around our coastline. The island is planning a gigantic festival to accompany the arrival of the ships. They will be in Lerwick for four days before they continue on.

Maybe I should be glad I am not going to be here. We would have a major traffic jam at the car-park with all of those tourists.

The Eshaness Tourism Director,
Sharma

Date sent: Sunday, 9 May 1999
Subject: **Puffin Alert from Shetland**
To: @LIST5E23.PML

It's happened. I went out after supper to check the sunset and the puffins have arrived. There are hundreds, probably thousands, of them swimming around the feet of the cliffs. They arrived some time this afternoon. Oh, how I hope some of them stay in this area. There is a colony of ten thousand of them at the south end of the island near the airport and some fifty thousand at the north on Unst. Some of them must want to stay in the nice homey cliffs of Eshaness.

All those birds swimming just offshore is an amazing sight. It blows my mind to think they have been swimming in the ocean all winter and now they are coming home. Ever since I wrote my children's book *Peadair's Rescue* I have been curious about what the puffins do in the ocean all winter. After some research on the subject I found out I am not the only one wondering. No one knows for sure where the puffins go or what they do. But, one thing for sure, they have arrived back home in Shetland.

In case you can't tell I am a little excited.

The Puffin Fan,
Sharma

Date sent: Monday, 10 May 1999
Subject: **Poor Gulls**
To: @LIST5E23.PML

Greetings,

It's finally started to rain at the lighthouse. The raindrops are not large but the wind is strong (forty miles an hour) so it's not so nice outside. The two seagulls which hang out on top of the garage have moved to the east side of the lighthouse seeking shelter with the lighthouse on one side and the sundial on the other. They keep shaking their heads trying to get dry. Gulls are not very smart birds

but since it is still raining, how do they think they can get dry?
Maybe they just are trying to get the rain out of their eyes. Rainfall
is forecast by the 'man in the little black box' to be in the vicinity
for the next two days off and on. I will try to get some short hikes
in-between showers. I certainly cannot complain since this is the
first rainy day in the ten I have been here.

I wonder if the puffins are still out there. The spectacle of all
those birds swimming at the bottom of cliff made me think someone had taken a crayon and drawn a bright yellow, red and black
ring around the shore. The ring was probably three feet wide,
maybe wider, and solid bird. Since distance is hard to judge from
the height of the cliffs it could have been wider. If the rain lightens
I will rush out to take a look. Maybe the rain convinced them they
should live in 'our' cliffs. I am worried they will go keep moving
on to the south end of the island or go north to Unst.

Charles Tait, one of Scotland's great photographers, is due
here today. We are going to take pictures at Eshaness and then
go to the Northern Isles of Yell and Unst. Charles and I have had
oodles of communication via e-mail but have never actually met.
His photography is remarkable. I use many of his pictures on
Scottish Radiance. On the first day I was to spend being a
tourist, what is it doing – raining. We are planning to visit some
of the other Shetland lighthouses. Many of his photographs are
to be used in my lighthouse book.

Rain means one thing for sure. I will get a lot of work done
on the novel before Charles arrives. Maybe that will make up for
the days I have been out running around in the hills. The lighthouse is a great place to write as no one interrupts you. But, it is
obvious I have to be disciplined in another way. The beauty of
the place constantly is drawing me outside. To sit at the computer
and juggle words does not compare with the birds, ocean and
sheer beauty of Eshaness.

The Struggling Writer

Date sent: Tuesday, 11 May 1999
Subject: **Day after the Storm**
To: @LIST5E23.PML

Greetings,

I am staring out my 'window on the sea', which is the south window of the dining room It got its name because whether I am
working or eating dinner I can see the sea. The sunshine is trying
to peek through the heavy cloud cover and I can see one sparkly
spot on the ocean. While I am waiting on water to heat on the
Rayburn for tea I decided I would get a short note off. Sorry,
I was late getting yesterday's note off. It did make me feel good
that many of you sent e-mails asking where my daily note was.

It will be a little marshy for me to walk this morning but I
am still going. I only have three days left at Eshaness. I want to
walk as much as I can. I am anxious to see our friends who live
in the Highlands but it will be hard to leave. If the weather co-
operates I want to walk the hills to Stenness since I was told
there are puffin nests in the lower cliffs along St Magnus Bay. I
am not sure I told you, but when I finally got out to check on
the puffins they had gone. Just like that.

To get to the place where the puffin nests are located it will
take me by the baby seals also. But!!! Just on the other side of
the loch near the baby seals the artic terns must have a nest. The
last time I was down there they were more than a little upset
with me. At first they just circled and made lots of noise. As I
kept going they started circling lower and swooping at me. I
decided it was time to change direction. As I mentioned before,
they are a very aggressive bird when it comes to protecting their
nest. I definitely do not want to leave here with wounds from
being pecked on the head by the artic terns. Most of the shep-
herds carry sticks to fight them off if their nests and the lambs
happen to be in the same area. They are not very big but they
are responsible parents. I believe from now on I will find a good
walking stick and wear a hat just in case I stumble into their
territory.

Because of the weather Charles Tait and I did not go up the northern most tip of Shetland yesterday. Our goal was a beautiful lighthouse on a rock just offshore called Muckle Flugga, which I definitely want to see before I leave. We are planning to go tomorrow. The weather is partly cloudy but later tonight we are supposed to have heavy rain and thunderstorms. I'll tell you more about that in a minute. Anyway I did some research for the trip to Unst tomorrow and the bird sanctuary is where the fifty thousand puffins live, so I am taking plenty of film. It is Shetland's largest puffin colony with some other small (?) ones having 'only' twenty thousand residents each. The Stenness colony is small with only around a thousand birds. If you do not hear from me tomorrow, all is well at the lighthouse and I am just off visiting fifty thousand puffins.

Yesterday's storm was my first. I learned some things. When it is going to rain all day I should stockpile coal inside. I had to go out in a downpour to get more coal. Not smart on my part, as even with my rain suit on I got soaked. Second, it is drafty around the windows. We have talked about putting in thermopane windows. That is definitely a good idea. Also another good idea is to apply plastic film inside the windows like we use on the farm. For the first time yesterday I was cold inside the house. When Tom arrived to check on me I had on two sweaters, plus my raincoat. First thing he inspected the Rayburn that happened to giving off good heat for a change. The problem was that with my laptop computer on the dining room table I'm between two windows and the drafts are horrible.

The wind howls around the tower. The solicitor in Lerwick had warned me so I would not be frightened the first time I heard it, but I actually had heard it before at Noss Head. It is not a horrible sound and it sort of lulled me to sleep last night. Not only could I see wisps of light from the beacon bouncing off the clouds through my window, but also I heard the tower howling. If I were superstitious I would think Eshaness was haunted with the funny swirling mist and noise of the wind. But it is just part of living at a lighthouse in a storm. As the light's attendant put it well. 'The best way to live at a lighthouse is to be outside when the weather is good but when the weather is bad make sure you have all your supplies so you can stay by a coal fire and read a book (or for me write a novel)'.

I am working on my novel today and cooking up some of the last things I brought out here. I have gotten good at cooking on the Rayburn and it is great. Today I am making bread and butter pudding with some leftover bread. I have a turkey breast to cook and if the fish van comes it will be tomorrow's meal. I have not heard from Tom whether he was able to tell the fish van driver to stop.

Sun just came out. Wonder how long that will last? It is supposed to be nice until late this afternoon when thunderstorms are likely to move in again. I have been postponing going to town because four hours in Lerwick in the rain doesn't sound like great fun. I have to go on Thursday no matter what. Tom wants to take me in but I am going to try to convince him I can take the bus. Sometimes I think he feels I can't take care of myself or, as Dean is always saying, I need a keeper.

A Rayburn Gourmet Cook,
Sharma

Date sent: Tuesday, 11 May 1999
Subject: **It is Heaven**
To: @LIST5E23.PML

Hi! It's Me Again!

The fish van was here. She simply pulls up to the gate and honks. The service is great. Such isolation I have at this light-house with food being delivered to my door and when I want to go to town the bus comes right to the gate.

The contents of the van were heaven. Freshly caught haddock, salmon, scallops, crabs, sea trout, plaice, and some fish I had never seen before were beautifully displayed. Plaice is one of my favorite fishes so that is what I am having for supper. Fresh plaice with a salad, some rice, and bread pudding. This is really roughing it. The fish van can bring me meat also but I am more interested in the fish. One plus is she also carries the common supplies people need like milk, butter and bread. A great help if I run short and do not want to go to Lerwick

It is has finally dawned on me that there are hundreds of people in Shetland who live in isolation like me at the lighthouse so an entire industry has developed around serving these people. I am sure the fish van does very well. Not only is it bringing the fish to people who live in remote areas but also it is supplying a market for the local fishermen's catch. Couldn't ask for more.

Yes, homesteading (my agent's term) at the lighthouse is really tough.

In the Wilderness,
The Well Fed Keeper

Date sent: Wednesday, 12 May 1999
Subject: **Oh! Me!**
To: @LIST5E23.PML

Hi! All!

Sad day. This will be my last day at the lighthouse for this trip. It is a glorious day with broken clouds making it sunny and gray and the colors are gorgeous. I will probably spend the whole day taking pictures and packing. There is not much to pack but Tom and I have to close all the shutters. He will turn the water off after I leave tomorrow. I have to defrost the freezer and clean out the refrigerator. That's it! I would wash the linens but since I do not have a washer the sheets and towels will have to stay dirty until I arrive back in September.

Yesterday's adventure with Charles Tait was fantastic.
We visited what are called the Northern Isles, Yell and Unst.
You ride a 'roll on – roll off' ferry twice to get to Unst. Our goal
was to see and photograph Muckle Flugga, one of the most
remote and beautiful lighthouses in the world. A member of the
famous Stevenson family designed it, just like Eshaness. We got
pictures but it was overcast so I am not sure how good they will
be. Yell is a rocky island and does not much appeal. Unst is
beautiful, there are big farms with cows and sheep and the
pastures go right down to the sea, which makes a tranquil scene.
The west side of the island is mountainous so when we climbed
to see the lighthouse we saw farms spread out below us
surrounded by the sea. I hope my pictures turn out, as it is an
extraordinary view. I have never seen anything like it before.

The people were so friendly. Charles was selling postcards so
we went to all the wee shops including the most northern post
office in Great Britain. After Unst there is no land until the
Arctic. It seems to me the people who live in such isolated places
tend to be among the friendliest people anywhere.

Charles spent about an hour photographing swallows that
were feeding on insects at a lochan. You could see the birds'
reflections in the water as they swooped in for their dinner. He
shot two rolls of film trying to capture the right angle. They
should be spectacular pictures. They were northern swallows
with black wings and bodies but white breasts. They had the
common forked tail.

Now as to the puffins! What can I say? Fifty thousand
puffins is a lot of birds. They probably haven't all arrived yet but
they were everywhere. The area is known for another bird called
bonxies. Bonxies (Great Skua) are huge birds with white under
their wings. They are as big as an eagle and not the least bit
friendly. They are so hostile and when you walk in the hills you
need a stick to chase them off. Somewhat like the Northern
Terns, but the bonxie will attack whether they have babies or
not. Do not be concerned when I say birds are aggressive. You

have to respect them just like the sea by being prepared and knowing their habits. Shetland is world renowned for its birds. They are in their natural territory and we, as visitors, must respect them. I liked the bonxies. The most astonishing treat was the beautiful lark we heard in the mountains when we were photographing the farms. Its song was exquisite but we never saw it. Charles said they are very tiny. In my mind I keep a list of special events that will never be forgotten and I have added our half hour in the mountains of Unst with the bonxies and the lark. It was a rare occasion.

I ate haddock for lunch and had sea trout for dinner. Oh my, what meals they were with the fish freshly caught and well prepared. I am having lobster with pasta tonight as Tom caught a small lobster that fits into my pan. He wanted it to be really fresh so I cooked it last night while he supervised. Maybe he just did not think I would cook it correctly. I will pick out the meat, put it in a cream sauce and serve it over pasta for my last lighthouse meal.

All I can say is, Dean and I really lucked out. Eshaness is a wonderful home with an elegant house and the beauty of the Shetland Islands thrown in. You add to that the genuine down to earth people and it is a total win-win situation.

Oh, I forgot the fishermen. They caught a five-pound brown trout in the loch behind us yesterday afternoon.

Got to run, Tom is here to take me to Lerwick to deposit my book check. This is the first BIG pay check I have received from writing. It is staying here in Scotland to take care of Eshaness.

I will probably write later tonight because my bus comes at 7:00 in the morning to get me to the plane.

Sadly,
The Lighthouse Keeper for One More Day

Date sent: Thursday, 13 May 1999
Subject: **All Good Things Must End**
To: @LIST5E23.PML

Hi! All!

All good things must come to end so new things can happen.
Tom will be here soon to lend a hand in shutting up the house. It
is sad time for me. I love this place, truly love it. It belongs to us
so it is only a short time until we can come back. For some reason I am having trouble holding on to that thought.

I'm really tired tonight. Tom's clutch stopped working on his
'wee white truck' just as we arrived in Lerwick. The 'wee truck'
is usually used only around Eshaness. He felt it might be easier
to find a parking place for it in Lerwick than if he drove his big
truck. Parking is a problem in Lerwick. Whatever was wrong
with the clutch that he couldn't fix it? After I did my banking we
decided to try to drive the truck home so Tom could fix it himself. I grabbed fish and chips to go for lunch. The problem
caused the truck to jerk violently when we started and when we
had to stop. I opened my fish and chips but by the time we had
gone a half-mile I wrapped them back up and put the package
on the floor. I needed to hold on to the seat tightly so I would
not fly into the windscreen. We thought we were going to get out
of Lerwick without a major problem. But, a hill just after the
Co-op roundabout did us in. We got only about a third of the
way up it and the truck stopped dead. Tom could not get it
started again. Cars were lined up behind us. We had no idea
what we should do. Being a friendly place three or four people
got out of their cars to help us. They pushed us off the road into
a car-park behind the roundabout. When most of the traffic had
cleared out we made another run at the hill and this time made it
to the top. Once outside town we drove 43 miles without being
able to change gears. It was a tense journey. Finally Tom decided
to have the Brae garage fix the truck. We went and got a cup of
tea while they soldered the clutch cable that had broken. It took

about an hour to get it fixed and then we drove home without another problem.

This is the last day and it is one of the most beautiful of all of them. It is just downright exquisite and so peaceful. Oops, here comes Tom so we can shut up everything. Gee, I hate to do this.

This is the end of the lighthouse letters for this trip. I may write something from the Scottish mainland. Otherwise I will touch base with you when I arrive back in the States.

And so the lighthouse keeper turns it over to our trusty caretaker, Tom. I am confident he will take good care of it for us, but it still did not stop the tears as I lay in bed staring out of the window watching the light beam go by.

Bye for now,

The Soon-to-be Off Duty Lighthouse Keeper

Date sent: Friday, 14 May 1999
Subject: **Killing Time**
To: @LIST5E23.PML

Hi, All

I have an hour before I catch my train to Aviemore to meet Robert and Margaret Macdonald, our friends from Skye, who now live in Grantown-on-Spey at Castle Grant Home Farm. I thought I could go by train from Aberdeen to Aviemore but I had to come to Inverness first. It works but it is just the long way round. I am sitting in a café in the Inverness train station drinking tea and typing away. Laptops are wonderful.

It is spring in mainland Scotland. Lilacs, fruit trees, gorse and rape are in full bloom. The countryside is a riot of color against a background of green. It is much more colorful than Shetland was. For those of you who are not familiar with it, gorse is an ugly bush with huge thorns. In the spring it blooms with bright gold flowers and literally trims the hillsides in gold. In contrast rape is a field crop grown for its oil. Rape fields are bright florescent yellow. From the air the ground looks like a florescent yellow royal coat bordered by dark green trimming glittering with gold.

The flight from Shetland was uneventful but I was hoping I might see a pod of Orca whales. I could see the water all the way but no whales.

Three things happened before I left the lighthouse that I want to share. Last night there was a gigantic rainbow with highly defined colors over St Magnus Bay. I hope I captured the intense colors as I shot another roll of film. My photographs so far have all turned out well. Tom and I stopped closing the shutters to stand and watch the rainbow until it disappeared.

This morning I saw an otter. The Shetland otter is bigger than other otters with a lighter brown pelt. He was playing on the edge of one of the voes. I did not see any others. This did not seem to bother him as he looked like he was enjoying himself. They are often caught by the Shetland people and kept for pets, or so someone on the bus told me.

Third, there is a huge population of hedgehogs on the islands. I have never seen one of these prickly little creatures in the wild. It will happen one of these days as I have been told they are everywhere on the islands. The one I saw today had strayed on the road and gotten killed. I had to ask someone on the bus what it was.

The lighthouse's windows are hidden behind wooden shutters again. It looked dismal and abandoned as I got on the bus. Tom is going to be an excellent caretaker. He loves the lighthouse and will inspect it often. His last words to me before I departed were he was pleased 'nice people like Dean and I' had bought the lighthouse.

Got to run, as it is time to catch a train. If all goes well Robert, Margaret, Sarah, and Jenny will be waiting at Aviemore. I say if all goes well, because last time we tried this, the cows decided to wander onto the road and Robert had to chase them so he didn't get to come.

Just a Tourist Again,
Sharma

PART FOUR

BACK IN THE USA

Date sent: Monday, 24 May 1999
Subject: **It's Awful!**
To: Susie@world.net

Susie,

I arrived back in the USA without a hitch. A miracle in itself as airlines are not known for being on time or functioning without some type of problem. (A bad attitude left over from my consulting days.) My visit with the Macdonalds was grand. The area around Grantown-on-Spey was stunning as always with the Grampian Mountains dominating everything. This time the mountains did not have on their snow bonnets.

Being on their farm has always been a joy but it seemed strange to not be able to go out of the door and see the ocean. When they first moved here I missed the ocean, which was so much a part of their farm on Skye. Then I came to love the area for its rugged mountains and beautiful valleys. Now just coming from the lighthouse I am back to missing the ocean. It is this combination of beautiful coastal scenery, mountains and gorgeous farms that makes Scotland such a treat to visit and so hard to leave.

For the last three days I have been up about 4:00 in the morning as I try to adjust back to the US Eastern Standard Time Zone. The good thing about jet lag on this end of the trip is you get a lot of things done in the morning. I have finally sorted through all of the mail and now am beginning to get caught up on the website material.

It is important for me to stay busy right now. My thoughts are stumbling around in a wilderness of confusion. It was wonderful to get back to Dean, the farm, Kiri, the cows and the chickens but something is missing. I yearn for the lighthouse and the ocean. It has always been difficult for me to leave Scotland

and return to the US. Maybe because I know it will be a long time before I return to the 'bonnie land'. This time I miss our new home with an ache difficult to describe. When I go out to hang up the clothes between the birch trees behind the barn I am longing to be at the rear of the lighthouse with the sea spread out in every direction. Believe it or not I even miss that contrary red Rayburn. That has got to be a sign of some kind of serious illness.

This is the first time in my life I have had two homes. Especially ones that are both so fabulous. I want to be at both of them. I did not realize how difficult it would be emotionally to have them four thousand miles apart. The cost of travel has always been an issue and had to be figured into the equation, but what was not considered was the pain involved with them being so far apart? A friend who has homes in Spain and in Scotland says you get use to it after awhile. Hopefully, he is right, but right now all I feel is distress. There have been tears when I think too much about the lighthouse. My self-prescribed medicine is to keep busy and try to forget it all.

We set the dates for our return trip in September. It has always helped me get over the pain of missing Scotland to schedule another trip. You ought to consider going with us since by then I hope to have furniture. It is my plan to start on the furniture hunt next week. I found some mail order places that deliver to Shetland and some do it without charge. When you get free delivery to Shetland you are really getting a bargain.

Homesick for Our Home with Light on Top,
Sharma

Date sent: Monday, 14 June 1999
Subject: **Moira Kerr's Song**
To: Susie@world.net

Susie,

Remember when we went to see Moira Kerr perform at the Highland Festival in Sarasota she talked about doing a song about our lighthouse if and when we ever got one. Moira, like you, never once doubted that we would eventually get our dream. She kept saying it would fall into place. She was right and it did. An e-mail arrived from Moira yesterday and she has written the song. It is entitled it 'Eshaness'. My eagerness to hear the song is eating me up. It is so severe I would jump on the airplane and fly over just to hear it. The album with the song on it is due out at the end of the month but the end of the month seems like a million years away to me.

How did I go from being an ordinary person who lives on the farm in the Midwestern part of the United States to being filmed by the BBC, writing a guidebook to Scotland, having a good friend who is a popular singer in Scotland, and now having a popular song written about her new home? It is more like a fantasy than reality.

The answer is that dreams are made, not something that just happens to you. Eshaness did not just happen; it took a lot of work and pain. Moira and I did not just happen, we worked at being friends. Well, the song is just a result of friendship which as you know is something I treasure and work hard everyday to enrich. It takes hard work to be a good friend.

You're Beloved Friend,
Sharma

Date sent: Monday, 21 June 1999
Subject: **Furniture Nightmare!**
To: Susie@world.net

Susie,

Things are more settled and my homesickness for the lighthouse is slowly disappearing. Probably because I am busy everyday working on stories related to the trip and planning the next trip.

I have ordered the first of the furniture. Believe it or not I found a sale on a custom made sofa and chair which could be delivered to the Shetlands free. Remember the website for the company in Wales I had you look at, that is where they are being made. The furniture prices in the UK are higher than in the US and that is without taking into consideration the exchange rate. The sofa and chair will be dark green to match the wallpaper in the living room. Actually it is not a sofa but a sofa-bed. If we ever have to list the lighthouse as self-catering I can say the facility will hold more people. You never know, we may have that many guests ourselves.

I would like to complete the furnishings so it is all over. Looking at our bank account though, all we may have is the bed I bought this spring and the two stuffed pieces from Wales. As I investigate the prices of things I begin to realize how much it is going to cost to furnish this house. Every time I look at the cost of things in the UK I thank God we did not buy a lighthouse with three houses to furnish. We would have been in debt for the rest of our life.

Anyway, if you come in September you will have a place to sleep, sit and watch TV.

The Long Distance Shopper,
Sharma

Date sent: Friday, 25 June 1999
Subject: **Happy Birthday To Me**
To: Susie@world.net

Sue,

The furniture list is complete. I am sure I am going to have a
nervous breakdown. I have only listed the bare necessities and it
is still horrendously expensive. I tell myself that once all of this
stuff is ordered it will be a nice comfortable home. Besides my
birthday is in two days so I can say I am giving myself early
birthday presents. Just what I always wanted for my birthday
this year was another microwave, a small portable stereo, a
bookcase, kitchen utensils, bedding, and the top of my wish list
definitely was another automatic washer. Yikes! The only item
on this list that was cheaper than a comparable piece of
equipment in the US was the automatic washer. They were out of
the model I ordered and substituted a better one for less money.
Submitting the order by phone I was concerned the girl was little
confused as I was ordering from the US for delivery in the UK.
Considering how big the order is I hope she does not get it
mixed up.

I am absolutely delighted you are coming in September.
I think I told you my brother and his wife will be there also.
They astonished me by wanting to stay the entire month. I will
be glad for the company and the opportunity of sharing the
excitement of everything that goes on at Eshaness.

Happy Birthday to Me,
Bankrupt Sharma

Date sent: Monday, 19 July 1999
Subject: **Shine on Me**
To: Susie@world.net

Susie,

Moira Kerr's album just arrived. I have waited so long to hear 'Eshaness' I put the CD in the player skipping to song number eight. Holding my breath I waited for the song to start. Then slowly a gentle rhythm started accompanied by words describing perfectly what lies deep within me. Moira's stunning voice describes exactly how I feel right now.

> Shine on Me
> Shine on Me
> How I miss you Eshaness so far across, so far across the sea.

Then the chorus has one more line added

> Shine on Me
> Shine on Me
> How I miss you Eshaness so far across, so far across the sea.
> How I love you Eshaness so far across, so far across the sea.

The tears rolled down my cheeks as I was set free for just for a few minutes from the emptiness I feel without our picturesque lighthouse home. Somehow the music brought the simple little house with its short tower closer. The lighthouse is still four thousand miles away but for just a few moments I was there. I do love it even though I know it is only a small building sitting out in the middle of nowhere.

I keep saying my sadness being away from Eshaness is easing but there are moments when it is like it just began. Any advice you have, please share it with me as I still have to live for the next ten years with only short visits to Eshaness.

Confused,
Sharma

Date sent: Tuesday, 27 July 1999
Subject: **The Furniture is Lost**
To: Susie@world.net

Sue,

Tom called this morning and nothing has arrived from the order
I submitted for the lighthouse household goods. So, I called the
company. The mail order firm has no record of the order. None!
An order costing over £3,000 has just disappeared. There have
been no charges to my credit cards so I don't think it is any type
of fraud. Those idiots have just lost my order. They say the problem is that I ordered through the UK division. Since I live in the
USA it probably was sent to the International Division. The
International Division does not handle UK orders so they probably sent it back or some such nonsense.

     To be perfectly honest I do not care how they lost the order
as long as they find it quickly. We are facing arriving at the
lighthouse without any of the basics that were in that order.
You and I could survive as we have the sofa-bed along with the
good bed I bought last spring, but what we will do when Ray
and Marylou arrive? The mail order firm is checking and I
should know in a couple of days when and if everything will be
delivered.

     I may have made a big mistake by using mail order instead
of waiting until I got to Shetland. It is just that everything in
Shetland is more costly than what I can get from the mail order
firm. Using mail order saved lots of money and that is an
important issue right now.

     Hopefully I will hear in the next couple of days that all is
well.

Worried,
Me

Date sent: Thursday, 29 July 1999
Subject: **Distraught**
To: Susie@world.net

Sue,

The UK mail order company finally acknowledged they cannot find my order and are sure none of it has been sent. I got so angry on the telephone I probably shocked them by becoming hysterical. I lost it completely. Sitting with phone in hand all I could do was sob.

For the first time since we bought the lighthouse I am thoroughly depressed and apprehensive about the wisdom of the purchase. If I cannot even acquire furniture for our new home how can we become good guardians of Eshaness? It is all so annoying. The distance is not the only problem, ways of doing business and cultural issues seem to be getting in the way also.

The mail order company wants me to send the order again and they will give it priority processing. This time I am submitting it in writing and sending it by e-mail to a supervisor. Hopefully, this will guarantee that it goes somewhere this time.

The bad news is you and I will have to function without most of the things while you are there. I am trying to be optimistic and think some of it might arrive before we get there but the mail order company did not give me much hope.

Frustrated and Disappointed,
Sharma

Date sent: Wednesday, 18 August 1999
Subject: **We have a Microwave**
To: Susie@world.net

Susie,

With less than three weeks until we get to Eshaness the first of the mail order items has arrived. We have a microwave.

There are other things in that order I wished would have gotten there first. We already have two other ways of cooking, electric stove and the Rayburn, so what comes first? The microwave. The good news is the system is starting to work; with one thing coming the other goods cannot be far behind. I thought everything would come together so Tom would not have to deal with a bunch of deliveries but each item is shipped separately from its manufacturer. Tom does not seem to mind that every day he has to look in his garage to see if anything new has been delivered. Shetland is so peculiar at times. They just drop my lighthouse deliveries in Tom's garage. I guess it is a well-known fact that he is our caretaker and everyone seems to know him.

I am getting more and more excited as the time to go to Eshaness is drawing nearer. It is almost time to start thinking about packing box number two. I wonder if a day will ever come that I will travel to Shetland without a box of household items as my second piece of luggage.

Hopeful,
Sharma

Date sent: Thursday, 26 August 1999
Subject: **Box For Trip II**
To: Susie@world.net

Susie,

Tom called and we now have a stereo at the lighthouse so we can bring CDs with us. You know how important music is to me. Last trip I played CDs on the laptop computer but it has horrible sound. The only things that have been delivered are the smaller items. Still no bed or washing machine has arrived.

Packing of the second box has begun. I do not have as many things to take this time. Dean is bringing a box when he comes so we can divide the load. This time I have some blankets, a few more dishes, some clothes I will leave there and coffee. None of us are real fond of UK coffee so I thought we could keep two pounds of Starbucks in the freezer. It is funny how little things that are really a matter of habit become larger in situations like this. Looking forward to my morning coffee is an important event in my day. When the coffee is not what I am used to it becomes disappointing. There is absolutely nothing wrong with UK coffee, it is just not what I am accustomed to. The issue of tea is totally a different story. I like Scottish tea better than ours so I drink a lot more tea in Scotland than at home. Constantly I caution myself not to make judgments about what it better or best but to understand it is a matter of what you are used to that makes the difference.

Don't forget to bring many layers of clothing as Tom says the weather can be extremely changeable in the fall. September is usually pretty dry and warm but since we are coming it will probably be wet and cold.

Packing,
Sharma

Date sent: Friday, 27 August 1999
Subject: **Video Production**
To: Susie@world.net

Susie,

It looks like I am going to be a television star. Lyle Morgan, a video producer has contacted me to schedule an interview while I am at Eshaness. They are producing a documentary on 'Scotland's Lighthouses', hopefully to be aired on United States Public Broadcasting. Their first request was to come to Eshaness to take footage of the sunset but they want to do it on the day I arrive. After much discussion I agreed to their filming the sunset the night I arrive but I made sure they understood that they could not interview me until the next morning when I had gotten a good night's rest. We will do the interview early in the morning so they can fly to Holy Island to film the lighthouse there. I do not know why these media people always want to interview me right after I have made that horrendous night flight to Scotland. First, the BBC did that and now Morgan Video. Do you think it could be a conspiracy?

Tom called and more of the little things for the lighthouse have arrived but none of the big stuff. He is concerned that I will have to struggle with my box and stuff on the buses so he is meeting me at the bus station in Lerwick and will take me to the Co-op for groceries and what ever else I need. He is always so kind and helpful.

Television's Next Star,
Me

Date sent: Thursday, 2 September 1999
Subject: **E–Day Trip II**
To: Susie@world.net

Susie,

I am ready to leave. Box number two is all packed and it isn't nearly as heavy as my first box. Maybe I am getting better at packing or I have less 'essentials'. I am as excited, as I was the first trip when I went to take possession of Eshaness in May. Hopefully that will never change and it will always be a big deal to me. What is gone is my anxiety about being alone. Having spent three weeks at Eshaness in May by myself makes me confident in my ability to handle whatever comes along out there. Second, this time I am only going to be alone for two days out of the whole month I am there.

Dean will spend his first extended amount of time at Eshaness. He keeps telling everyone he has spent only five hours there and that was before we bought it. His time estimate might be a little off but it is definitely true he has not been there overnight. The most important time to be at a lighthouse is at night when the light is on. Otherwise it is just a house by the sea.

Will be putting the computer on e-mail forwarding so you can use this address to reach me. I will e-mail as soon as I arrive to let you know how things went. You arrive only one day later so you might not even have time to see my e-mail.

See You at Eshaness Soon,
Sharma

PART FIVE

THE SECOND TRIP – SEPTEMBER IN SHETLAND

Date sent: Friday, 3 September 1999
Subject: **Arrived Early**
To: @LIST5E23.PML

The flights were uneventful and the best part was that I could see the ground the entire way from Aberdeen to Sumburgh. You fly over one island after another. It was unique to see all of the different islands among the slate gray sea without any white caps at all.

I got into Shetland a few minutes early. Tom and I had a slight miscommunication. We had agreed to meet at the bus station at 3:00 pm. When I got to the bus station Tom wasn't there. This was so unlike him I was really worried something had happened. I waited and waited. He still had not shown after half an hour. I did not know what to do. I needed to get groceries so I decided to leave my box and suitcase with the station attendant and go to the Co-op. That way, whether Tom came or I took the bus I would be able to eat for the next few days. Just as I got my possessions stored in the bus station back room an older couple came up and asked if I had seen a friend of theirs. From their description I remembered the person being on the plane. They were supposed to have met her at the airport and they were a few minutes late and we were a few minutes early so somehow they had missed each other totally. I told them she had not come on the airport bus with me. I mentioned I had also missed my connection. They laughed and said Tom was down at the main bus stop frantically looking for a gray haired American lady. He had been there for an hour and I had not shown up. They kindly volunteered to walk the two blocks and tell him where I was. When Tom still had not shown up after fifteen minutes I was just starting down the street to the main bus stop when I saw him drive up the street. I waved. He saw me but because of traffic he had to go around the block before he could drive into the bus station.

Being Tom, he was distressed because we had missed each other but I said no harm done. We loaded up my stuff and took off for the Co-op for groceries. With Tom's supervision I stocked up on groceries and we took off for Eshaness. The only real concern we had was the television film crew would be at Eshaness waiting for us when we arrived

It was a magnificent day with lots of sunshine and a beautiful sky full of fluffy white clouds. The colors have changed since spring when it was green with bright yellow flowers; now it is brown with fields of golden barley and many grasses among the start of the heather bloom. The hills will soon be ablaze with the royal purple of heather. The lowlands did not have as much heather but they had waving brown grasses.

We stopped at the Brae's store to get some of the wonderful soft rolls they sell. There is a fantastic bakery on Unst that delivers to the Brae Store. I always stock up on their baked goods when I shop in Brae. The freezer could use a dozen extra rolls with all the company I was having this trip.

Tears came to my eyes as we turned off the Hillswick Road and started down the Eshaness road. There were Da Drungs with their pointed heads sitting in St Magnus Bay. A little farther along we could see Dore Holm; the dinosaur shaped stack, standing in the water. Every time I see Dore I am even more overjoyed that I wrote my children's story 'Dore Holm' and made this piece of rock into a kind creature that saves whales. After we passed Dore I got my first glimpse of the lighthouse in the distance. I squealed at Tom, 'There it is'. I am sure he was thrilled as he sees it every day.

The film crew had not arrived so we unloaded my groceries and luggage. I was literally like a child at Christmas going from room to room inspecting all of the mail order items that had arrived. Tom had unpacked most of them and put them in the

appropriate room. (What would I do without Tom?) There were
a couple of boxes just arrived that I would unpack later after I
got the groceries put away and my box unpacked.

Just as I was finishing putting food in the freezer I heard
someone say, 'I hear an American accent'. The film crew had
arrived. They walked into total chaos. Nothing except the food
had been put away. Boxes were everywhere. I was apologetic but
they were delighted. They wanted me to leave some of the boxes
until morning so they could get pictures of me unpacking them.
As tired as I was, I would not have a problem with that.

Instead of working on the mess inside I showed them around
the outside, which gave me an excuse to check out the blowhole
and the cliffs. The sun was beginning to set and it looked like it
would be a magnificent sunset. The cameraman was concerned a
cloudbank that has just appeared above the horizon would spoil
the sunset. They said they wanted to explore the cliffs and take
some pictures so I went inside and made sandwiches for Tom
and I. Just as we were finishing our tea the film crew asked if
I would come out and pose for some pictures. It seems that
the cloudbank had given the sunset a different look with the
light being reflected around it. They placed the camera so they
could get the tower with the light on, sunset in the background,
and my silhouette at the front.

We made an appointment for early the next morning and
they took off for the St Magnus to get supper, as the hotel would
soon quit serving. Tom left soon after they did and I tried to at
least finish unpacking my box. All I want to do is take a bath
and go to bed so I will write more tomorrow.

Exhausted,
Sharma

Date sent: Saturday, 4 September 1999
Subject: **Washing Windows for** TV
To: @LIST5E23.PML

Greetings All,

This morning was spent with the film crew taking pictures of me washing windows of all things. Every star wants to start as a window washer in a strong wind. My hair was being unprofessionally arranged by the Shetland winds and it must have been just lovely. In total I spent five hours with them. Three hours last night and another two hours this morning. I hope the footage turns out okay. Shetland could not have provided a better day for video with beautiful puffy clouds and enough wind to make the waves crash on the cliffs into big foam.

After the film crew left I spent most of the day arranging furniture and the new items the way I wanted them. Tom helped me move things around. After much debate I decided to turn the room with the Rayburn into a combination living and dining room. This meant that Tom and I moved all of the new soft stuffed furniture from the living room to the Rayburn room. He was really tolerant of my changing my mind. (Dean would have been upset to say the least. He probably wouldn't even have done it.) The house looks nice except for one empty bedroom. Two absolute essentials are missing. The automatic washer and the electric kettle have not arrived yet. The little house is a lot more settled than I thought it would be when the mail order company lost my order.

Susie arrived without a problem using the bus from the airport. We had shepherd's pie made with mince, covered with mashed Shetland potatoes and topped off with Orkney cheese for dinner. After we ate we were going to watch the sunset but the fog moved in and the sunset was hidden behind heavy mist. We settled for watching the tower turn on. It was spectacular with the light rays in the dense fog.

I have not had time to see any wildlife. Tomorrow we will walk down to see the seals. Bad news! The television crew told me they think the puffins have departed for the open sea but maybe I can find a 'hanger on'.

The fog is starting to lift. That happened last night. After the fog withdrew we got an impressive sunset with enough clouds around to make interesting shapes. Sue was too tired to wait as she went to bed early. It's that night flight.

Sharma and Susie

Date sent: Sunday, 5 September 1999
Subject: **The Rayburn Gets Even**
To: @LIST5E23.PML

Greetings All,

The fog left last night only to return this morning along with a little rain so this may be a day to stay inside and read books. As I look out the window it does look like it is going to clear. Who knows this close to the ocean?

I didn't tell you how the Rayburn got even for all of the nasty things I have said about it. Those of you who have been getting my little epistles from Eshaness since May's trip know the biggest obstacle I have in living here is spelled RAYBURN. That darn stove and I just seem to have a major battle going on. This morning it took three fire-starters and two bundles of driftwood before it decided to burn. Well, that's nothing compared to what happened yesterday.

The first night when Tom and I arrived we tried to start the Rayburn but all we got was black smoke billowing out of the ovens all over the sitting room. We tried everything we could think of but ended up with the kitchen table being smoked and sooty. After talking to the Rayburn dealer it was diagnosed as a problem in the chimney. Trusty Tom unlocks the ladders from

their storage table in front of the lighthouse, drags them over to
the building and up on the roof he goes. Only to find he couldn't
sweep the chimney since its top is enclosed with only two small
vents on the sides. He couldn't decide whether to break the cap
free so I (yes, me) went up on the roof with him to see. Since I
know nothing about chimneys I did not think I would be a lot of
help. I have never been on a roof before in my life. When you
are on the roof it is easy to tell this lighthouse is two hundred feet
above the water. The view was majestic. (Another day I will have
Tom help me and go back up to take pictures.) Well, back to the
problem of the Rayburn. We definitely could not sweep the chimney from the top. Our next idea was to see if we could do anything through the hole that connects that cantankerous stove to
the chimney in the dining room. When Tom started digging into
that hole he found it was completely blocked with soot and three
dead birds. What a mess! Tom was covered with soot before he
was done. It wasn't long until we could feel cold air coming down
the chimney. Finally, it was clear. We started the fire again and
miracle of miracles the smoke went up the chimney not into the
room. One victory for humans and one loss for the Rayburn in the
Eshaness Lighthouse fight for control of the heating. Just checked
and it is burning brightly and sending a nice warmth into the
room. Today it must carry out its duties since it is cooking a large
beautiful Scottish chicken. It cooks meat without drying and yet
the roast is browned to perfection. Susie and I will have a wonderful Sunday dinner thanks to the pig-headed stove.

The other thing I did not talk about were all the things the
Morgan people had me do for the video footage. I think I mentioned I was washing windows. But doing it from the ground
was not good enough so up on a ladder I went with my hair and
raincoat blowing in a strong Shetland wind. Thank goodness
they did not ask me to go up on the roof. They had me typing at
my computer, which made me nervous so I made all kinds of
mistakes. They asked tons of questions. I must have not stuttered
too much because we didn't have to redo any of them. It is good

thing the Rayburn was not working or they would have filmed that battle. In their opinion the best footage was taken at sunset when I walked in front of the building. They looked at it later and said it is awesome and goose bumpy kind of stuff.

Tom refused to be filmed, but they were clever. By moving the cameras back when they were filming me washing windows they caught Tom on the roof trying to resolve the chimney problem. I do hope that footage turns out as he was wearing his traditional Shetlander blue work coverall and it documents how hard he works helping me.

The sky is getting lighter and if my new assistant keeper, Susie, gets up pretty soon we will be off on a visit to the local neighbors – the seals. Hopefully the white babies that were here in spring will be all grown up, grays like their parents, and romping around on the rocks or in the water.

Speaking of neighbors, the blankety-blank sheep got in the yard this morning. I must not have gotten the gate closed when the bus brought Susie last night.

My porridge is ready so I am going to have breakfast.

The Keeper
Sharma

Date sent: Monday, 6 September 1999
Subject: **Essentials**
To: mistysteak@world.net

Hubby,

Forgot, we do not have enough silverware for six people. You need to bring more of Mom's silver that is in the chest in the corner under the clock in the kitchen. It may be tarnished so use the silver cleaner under the sink to make it sparkle.

As we may have some neighbors in for tea could you also bring the Bed and Breakfast high tea dishes? You will find them in the cabinet in the dining room. In case you do not remember they have flowers on them with pink trimming. Bring as many of those as you can, as we will use them when our human neighbors visit.

A few apples would be nice so I could make a pie for Tom and you out of 'our' apples. Any thing else you can think of, throw it in. Might as well not waste the box space.

That's it for this trip or at least at this point. I just wanted you to have as big a box as I did. (Grin).

Wifey

Date sent: Monday, 6 September 1999
Subject: **Susie Sees the Sights and Meets the Neighbors**
To: @LIST5E23.PML

Greetings,

The weather seems to be setting a pattern. Fog rolls in from the south every evening about sunset. We have not had great sunsets the last two nights. The sunsets are interesting because of the clouds and fog but they do not flame like the ones I saw in May. It rains during the night. When we wake up it is misty and gray. About 9:00 am the sky starts to clear and by noon it is beautiful and sunny.

As soon as it started to clear yesterday Sue and I took off to visit the seals down at what I have been calling the 'seal rocks' but is actually a group of small islands called Bruddans. The surf was definitely smashing around so we shot two rolls of film each. The most impressive thing about the surf was its color, a beautiful shade of pale jade green, and as the waves rolled over they glistened like an emerald. We were only going to walk a short distance but ended up spending the whole morning taking surf pictures. That is one of the splendid things about Eshaness. You are never bored. There are so many things to do and each is a pleasure that can take all day.

This morning when we got to the Bruddans we found seals swimming in the water with only a big fat bull on the rocks. The big guy did not seem to have enough energy to get in and swim with the rest. Lazy we thought. We found a nice flat comfortable rock and watched the seals for a while. Another amenity of Eshaness is a huge selection of chairs. You find the nearest rock and sit down. Needless to say we are tired and sore from all of our hiking.

Yesterday we spent the afternoon putting furniture together and reading, accompanied by classical music on a BBC station we found on the new stereo. It was a pleasant Sunday and the Rayburn performed well cooking a scrumptious roast chicken. It cooks splendidly; if only it was as co-operative in starting. When I sit down to a delicacy cooked in the Rayburn I almost get over feeling it is the enemy here.

Speaking of the Rayburn, Tom brought us a bag of peat from his supply. He digs his own the old-fashioned way with a tusker. Burning some last night we found it creates a strong radiant heat and smells wonderful. I am either going to dig my own peat next year or buy some. I would like to dig it and Tom is willing to teach me. It is hard work so I will need to get on a strict exercise program a long time before I make the next trip.

The forecast is for rain all day but it looks like it might clear. Our agenda for today is hiking to the cemetery and maybe on to Stenness beach since we need to pick up some more driftwood for starting the Rayburn. Important announcement – the Rayburn did not go out last night using peat. We only have a little peat so most mornings it will be out. Also, when no one is here to tend it during the day it goes out so we need the wood. Also today I have to go put the trash out. Now there's a homey activity that makes me fell like a real native. The council truck picks up on Monday. We may seem isolated if you look at a map or pictures but we have services like water and trash just like a city.

If it does rain I will curl up with a good book. I have caught a bad cold and don't feel one hundred per cent. You never know what you will catch when you are shut up in an airplane for eight hours and the air is being recycled. I doubt if the system takes viruses and germs out during the recycling process.

I am not deathly ill but my nose is running and stuffed up. If it doesn't get better I will go to see the doctor who is only a few miles away. If I get really sick she does make house calls so we will have her come here. House calls by doctors are something which almost does not exist in the US today.

The rain has come and gone all day. Sue and I have read books and both of us took a nap. Big day – maybe not the way some people would look at it but it meant contentment for us. I actually put together a bedside table for the spare bedroom. That is quite an accomplishment for someone who can't drive a nail straight. The rest of the furniture, except for the big stuff, arrived today. I have a corner desk to put together on Wednesday. Maybe I should wait until Dean gets here since he is much better with a hammer than I am. The big furniture arrives on Wednesday so we should be totally settled in by Wednesday evening. The rooms look really cozy and it feels much more like a home now. Moving the couch and chair into the Rayburn room made a pleasant living/dining room. We find we are spending all our time there.

The master bedroom is completely furnished. On Wednesday the spare bedroom will join the ranks of the completed. My office will have only have a desk and a chair for now. Eventually I will add bookshelves and pictures to make it look more lived in.

Tomorrow Sue and I are off to Lerwick on the bus to pick up the last odds and ends needed to make this place a home. Essential things like a couple of wastebaskets, more light bulbs, bath mat, scissors, and mixing bowls. The little things everyone needs and are necessary but the hardest to remember to purchase.

Yesterday Sue and I decided to put a light bulb in the one lamp we had not set up. Since it was raining and we could not go outside we had plenty of time. It is good we had all of that extra time. I spent almost two hours trying to figure out how the bulb fit through the shade. Sue got tired of listening to me grumble about it and asked if she could give it a try. She tried for another hour until the poor lamp, after all of our pushing and shoving, broke. Not knowing whether we had broken it or there was something wrong with it we asked our resident expert on everything – Tom. He immediately screwed off something and within a minute had it all together. Tom is so quiet. He has not said so but I wonder if he thinks I am some kind of idiot. I can't put furniture together nor do something as simple as put a bulb in a lamp. Light bulbs are different over here. They pop in instead of screw into place. Sue and I roared with laughter over two intelligent women who could not put in one light bulb.

Since it rained the only wildlife report for the day is that the sea gull that lives on top of the garage is back. All of you who got my journal entries last spring remember the sea gull that was mating on the garage. Well, he is still here except no x-rated behavior to report. Once again he just sits and waits. Since he usually shows up about dinnertime I'm sure he is the one the former owners fed and made a pet. We will not feed him. He has a whole ocean of fish to eat.

Speaking of fish we will miss the fish van's arrival tomorrow so we are going to try to go to the fishmonger in Lerwick and get our fish instead. I love the fish van. It is such a delight for someone from the Midwest to have access to all of that fresh fish which comes right to my door.

That's all for today except that I love peat!! It is great in the Rayburn and we are going to look for a source so we can get enough to last the rest of this trip.

Sharma
The Keeper

Date: Tuesday, 7 September 1999
Subject: BBC **Shetland**
To: mistysteak@world.net

Dean,

It would be so exciting if WJR allows you to broadcast your
weekly radio program from Shetland. I talked to the main
producer at BBC Shetland and they are definitely interested.
Your producer should call or e-mail either BBC Shetland's head
producer or his assistant. She can contact them by either e-mail
or telephone. The man I talked to indicated he would check with
his superiors to make sure it was okay. It is important that WJR
tell them exactly what you would need. He described the studio
as small but brand-new. Definitely he wanted you to come see
him while you are here even if you do not do a broadcast this
trip. You could go see the studio between buses when we go into
Lerwick.

One of the things we wanted our retirement to include was
your broadcasting from Shetland, so this is especially exciting.
It makes it seem like it will be only a short while until we can
spend major blocks of time over here.

The Broadcaster's Wife,
Me

Date sent: Tuesday, 7 September 1999
Subject: **The Gales are Coming**
To: @LIST5E23.PML

Hi! All!

The first sizeable storm of this trip is to arrive tonight with
winds of up to gale Force 8 – 9. I am looking forward to it; this
will be the first extensive storm I have encountered since we took
possession of Eshaness. You might think this a little on the
weirdo side but storms are sensual and exciting. This lighthouse

has stood up to many so I am sure it can handle a few more. We will just have to stay inside until it passes

The ocean framed in the window in front of me has gigantic waves already and it is just starting. The sky is hazy with the sun peeking through the clouds but no rain yet. Actually except for the wind it is a nice day. Hanging clothes on the clothesline would not be a wise move today, as they would end up in the ocean for sure. The sound of the wind and the sea are hair rising. I feel safe sitting in this sturdy house listening to classical music on the radio and the storm's roar. A masterful symphony with wind, sea and a flute sonata is being presented just for us.

Sue and I walked to the cemetery this morning to see the ancient kirk. We disturbed the sheep in the fields along the road. Eventually Sue and I were herding twenty five sheep down the lighthouse road. This could have been the first sheep jam in Eshaness history caused by Americans with cameras. A car could not have gotten by us. Eventually the sheep gave up and jumped off the road to go back to munching on the grass. Just before we reached the cemetery road we saw another long line of sheep on the other side of the cattle grate near the Stenness road turn off. They were not on the road but crossing from one side to the other. It was quite a sight with St Magnus Bay and Da Drongs in the background with the bright green grass broken only by a fat white line of sheep. Our cameras clicked nonstop. It was only after we took the pictures that we noticed Tom's truck parked at the side of the road. Seeing Tom in among the sheep, we continued beyond the cemetery to say 'Hi'. Tom explained he was moving his sheep to a more sheltered area since the storm was coming. With the idea of the storm being imminent we hurried back to the cemetery and took our pictures. The old Kirk has antique writing on it surrounded and often covered with moss. I wondered how long it had been sitting on this hill over looking St Magnus Bay. The cemetery is a combination of well-tended old graves and modern tombstones. Col James, who owned the lighthouse before Dean and I, is buried there. I can understand why. The cemetery has a magnificent view and feels so connected to Eshaness. Maybe when my time comes I will join him on this hill.

Tom just took off with Sue for a sightseeing tour of Brae and Ronas Hill. Sue wanted to get some more pictures of the area and the beautiful rock formations in the sea including Da Drongs and Dore Holm. Time goes so fast at Eshaness it doesn't seem possible that Sue only has a few more days of her visit left. I sent a grocery list with them, as they will be near Brae. Whenever anyone goes near a grocery you have him or her get anything on the lighthouse grocery list since it is a few miles to the nearest store.

While I am on the subject of food, we had fresh haddock from the fish van last night. We were in Lerwick but Tom purchased the fish for us. I broiled it to just the right texture so it was neither dry nor slimy. It was brilliant. Tonight we are having mackerel that Tom caught yesterday. I do not know what to expect since I have never had fresh mackerel. Of course, Tom gave me instructions on the exactly how to cook it.

Yesterday's trip to Lerwick was a huge success except we got soaked in a sudden downpour. Not so good for someone with a bad cold. Hopefully it won't make me worse. I feel pretty good right now. My time is so precious here I do not want to spend some of it in bed with a cold.

In Lerwick we spent some time at the library. In their special Shetland Room they have some rare books by Amelia Barr, a Shetland writer that I have recently found and really like. Back home I bought two of her first editions and need three more to complete her Shetland series. Eventually I will bring them over here. Most of the Shetland books were written in the late 1890s. The library also had an extremely rare book on Shetland light-houses, which is so valuable that it is locked up in a vault. They are going to let me look through it during my next long visit to town. I have to warn them in advance so they can bring it to the library. Next trip to Shetland I will include time to do research at the library.

Two hilarious episodes occurred yesterday. Sue and I bought groceries for the next four days. With Ray and Marylou coming tomorrow, and Dean on Friday, we are talking about a lot of food. Our groceries took up most of the package space on the big bus. When we got to the minivan that brings us to the light-house we filled it with groceries and passengers had to sit on top of each other. Yes, I know I sent another list with the two going to Brae two days ago but when you start from nothing it takes a lot of groceries to feed five people.

The other incident may not be as amusing. Sue was out chasing sunset pictures last night. I was delighted for her because the fog had robbed her of many sunsets. Last night was an out of the ordinary night for photographs. There were pink and blue clouds along with beacons of yellow from the sun. I had not seen a sunset like that. I wonder how many different types of sunsets I will see here? They always seem to be different. We didn't eat until 8:30 pm, as she kept on taking pictures every time another masterpiece appeared. Unfortunately she was so into the photography she tripped and fell. Nothing major, just a little muddy and a slight sprain to her ankle. Sue likes Shetland so much Tom is helping her look for a wee croft house near here. If she could find one and restore it she would be happy.

Got to eat my lunch as the last of the furniture came in on the boat this morning and will be here around 2:00 pm. Probably better make something for Tom and Sue as they will be breezing in soon as Tom is needed to help the furniture people.

The Lighthouse Keeper

Date sent: Wednesday, 8 September 1999
Subject: **Gales Are Still With Us**
To: @LIST5E23.PML

Good Morning,

Strong winds are still with us but it is clear and sunny. A few
minutes ago we went out to take pictures and the waves were
gigantic. Yesterday it rained and the wind blew almost all day.
Right in the middle of the worst of the storm they delivered my
automatic washer and bed for the spare bedroom. It was difficult
to get the furniture in the house with such high winds. The
washer has a huge dent in its side that probably occurred as they
tried to get it through the door. It will be replaced but if it works
we will use it until then. Tom hooked it up but we need a rubber
washer before we can operate it. I am finding that in a remote
location like this you need to be prepared and have a supply of
miscellaneous paraphernalia like washers around.

The furniture is here and the house is set up. As I reflect on
what I have been through to get this furniture I cannot believe it
is all here. I am writing this in my office on a desk so I now have
no excuse not to go to work. No more exemption because of
needing the kitchen table for other things. I put the desk together
with my two little hands. Tom had put most of the small pieces
together but I decided I could put the desk together. It took me a
long time to figure how it was organized and then even longer to
screw in the bits and pieces needed to hold it together. I was so
proud of it. Tom walked in to see my pride and joy. His
comment was 'That one piece is wrong side out'. The worst part
was he was right! I have one side in backwards. Guess what?
It is staying backwards. The desk works and I do not care that it
has one piece backwards.

Sue and Tom managed a few hours sightseeing yesterday
without rain. She got some good pictures then something
happened to her camera and it wouldn't work. She found she had
completed a roll of film and that was the reason the shutter
wouldn't flash.

Ray and Marylou arrive today if the gales don't delay the planes. If the winds keep up they will arrive tomorrow with Dean. The gales are supposed to die down later today followed by a beautiful weekend. It was weird. About nine o'clock last night the wind just quit. It was still most of the night but the wind was back again this morning.

I fried Tom's fresh mackerel for dinner last night and it was wonderful. Rolling it in flour I fried it to a crusty brown. There is such a difference between fresh fish and what you buy at the store. I could just live on fish while we are here. It also helps to have someone catch it for you.

The plan for this morning is to brave the winds and get some pictures since it is clear and sunny. Hopefully we will do some washing once Tom gets the washer going.

The Rayburn is burning fine for a change. Maybe I have learned how to do it.

The Keeper

Date sent: Thursday, 9 September 1999
Subject: **Ray and Marylou's Arrival**
To: @LIST5E23.PML

Greetings From Sunny Shetland,

The wind has calmed down a little. Sue and I were out bright and early taking pictures of the surf. Such surf it is. The center of the storm has passed but it must take the ocean a while to settle. The waves hit the rock so hard they splash to the top of Moo Stack. It is colossal. The area around the seal rocks was misty with sea spray and our glasses were coated with salt. In an area called 'the cannon' the surf gets trapped in a rock cavern and each strong wave rumbles just like a cannon burst as it hits the wall. It was loud and frightening. Needless to say there were no seals swimming or sitting on the rocks. Actually there were no rocks as they were lost under the tumbling and foaming surf. It was amazing.

Just after we got back Tom arrived and wanted to take Sue down to see Stenness beach as the surf was so strong that it covered the entire beach. Sue grabbed her camera and off they went while I made a big pot of beef stew to put in the slow cooker for dinner for our guests tonight.

Sue and Tom arrived back. Sue was excited and ordered me to get my camera and take a couple of minutes to run down to Stenness with Tom. I am so glad I did. It was unimaginable. The surf was climbing up the sides of Stenness Island and Eshaness Skerry and breaking into clouds of mist. The angry water dashed across the beach and onto the grass. If I ever had any doubt of the strength of the ocean before this trip to Stenness, I don't anymore.

When I got back Sue, Tom and I had lunch and sat over a cup of tea and biscuits and discussed the surf. It seems at Eshaness we never lack topics of conversation. The other major topic was whether Ray and Marylou would make it into Sumburgh in such strong winds. The plan was to call the airport later in the afternoon and see if they have any information on their plane. When I talked to them earlier they had no idea of the status of the afternoon planes.

Evening arrived and I went out to wait for Bertie and the bus. I saw the bus go down Stenness Road but it did not come up to the lighthouse. I called the airport and the plane was in, so where were Ray and Marylou? Without a car there was nothing Sue and I could do but wait. A little bit later someone knocked on the door. It was Ray. They had taken a taxi all the way from the airport to Eshaness. They said their taxi driver had been an excellent tour guide and the cost wasn't outrageous. I was so relieved to see them. Staying in Lerwick for the night would be disappointing when you planned on being at a lighthouse.

After getting them settled into the spare bedroom with the new bed, Sue and I had them put on their coats again. We dragged them outside to see the cliffs and the tower before it got dark. I imagine they would have preferred a glass of wine and dinner first but if we did that it would be dark and they could not see anything. Naturally it never occurred to me that we would have many more days to look around but I was so proud of the lighthouse I wanted to do it right away.

Dean has now left the States and is on his way here. Whoopee!

The Lighthouse Inn Keeper,
Sharma

Date sent: Friday, 10 September 1999
Subject: **The Laird's Arrival**
To: @LIST5E23.PML

Greetings from the Lighthouse Crew,

After all of us had a good night's sleep and ate a hearty breakfast of porridge, we took off to see the countryside. Since today is Sue's last full day at the lighthouse we let her choose today's itinerary. She chose going to see the seals and then, if we felt up to it, walking to Stenness beach over the hills.

The surf was still high so Ray was able to get some great pictures of the surf around the Bruddans and the two islands off Stenness. I was really touched when my brother said he knew it would be beautiful here but not THIS beautiful. We did not see any seals as the surf was still over most of the rocks. The ocean was so spectacular on that side of the peninsula we decided to walk to Stenness. It is not far for the seagulls but the voes cut into the beach so humans have to walk around their long fingers, which probably doubles the walking distance. What a hike it was! The surf was crashing around in the many caves hidden in the cliffs so it was electrifying and salty. Every so often one of us would squeal with delight as a huge wave climbed over the top of the cliffs on Stenness Island. I was thankful Tom was not out checking his lobsters since all of his pots are between Stenness Island and Eshaness Skerry.

As we got nearer Stenness a fence that enclosed one of the croft's fields blocked our path. Frustrated, we could see the road to Stenness but had no idea how to reach it. Ray spotted a weakened place in the fence so we decided to try crossing there. With a great deal of effort we were able to struggle over it. Once in the field we walked toward a gate that would lead to the road. Here I am again without my map. A lot of good it does on the table back at the lighthouse. Repeatedly I have left behind the map and the guidebook with everything listed that should be seen. I should put them in my pocket and just keep them there.

When we finally reached the Stenness road we had a choice, whether we wanted to walk on further to the beach or go on back to the lighthouse. Once again we left it up to Sue. She chose going to the beach even though she was in a great deal of pain from the ankle she had sprained a couple of nights ago. Sue and I were a little disappointed, as the beach was not as spectacular as it had been when the storm first appeared. All of us were tired so we sat down on a log and just watched the surf and let the silence of the area settle around us. Stenness is a fascinating place with some buildings remaining from the time when the herring boats used it as a port. One of my favorites is a stone building covered with lichen and moss which no longer has a roof. It has such character. Maybe I will be able to convince Ray to paint a picture of this building with the beach in the background someday. Ray very seldom does pictures by request since he likes to paint only what moves him.

After resting at Stenness we started for the lighthouse. By then we were all tired and it seemed like a long way to a cup of tea. It is an easy walk because you are on the flat surface of the road until you reach the steep hill just before the car-park and the lighthouse. I was not sure I was going to make it up that hill but I did. I did not ask any of the others how they felt about it but I would not be surprised if they had as much or more trouble than me.

As soon as we hit the house we put the kettle on. The one thing which still has not arrived from the lost mail order is the electric kettle. My plain teakettle takes a long time to heat on the electric stove. The Rayburn is faster but it had gone out since we had neglected it for such a long time.

Since it was Sue's last day Ray spent the afternoon painting a watercolor picture from one of her photographs so she could take it home. It turned out beautifully and she was truly touched.

Tom delivered lobsters for our evening meal. Our plan from the beginning had been to have lobsters for the one meal we were all going to be together. We thought we would have to have something else since the sea was too rough for Tom to attempt to go to get the lobsters. Actually I was a little put out with him about his going out in the boat to get the lobsters in such high seas. I was positive he had endangered his life for our dinner. He assured me he had not taken any risks but I am still not sure I believe him.

It was soon time for the bus to come and I was so afraid that it would go down the Stenness road and not come to the light-house like it had the night Ray and Marylou came. This time I saw the white minivan turn up the lighthouse road so I ran and opened the gate. Sure enough 'The Laird', as Dean had started calling himself, had arrived at Eshaness Lighthouse. Lighthouses don't have Lairds but Dean announced that Eshaness did. In his hand he had a bag containing three bottles of well-aged whisky that he had bought in the Aberdeen airport for the lighthouse. As if a lighthouse needs whisky. I was thrilled to see him since this was the first time we had both been at the lighthouse since we bought it.

We got him settled and then the Scotch drinkers opened those precious bottles while I began preparing our lobster feast. First big problem was the lobster pot I had purchased was too small for five big lobsters so I had to use one borrowed from Tom. Second, we had no tools by which to crack the claws and pick the meat from the lobsters. Dean went out to the tool shed and came back with a spare piece of marble counter-top, a hammer and a couple of pliers, which we washed and made sterile. After the lobsters were steamed we turned the kitchen over to the guys to crack the shells and get the now bright red things ready for the table. Somehow with the reinforcement of Dean's scotch they were able to get the lobsters open enough that we could handle the rest on our plate at the table.

What a meal that was! The lobster was the best I had ever eaten. It was extremely sweet and not the least bit fishy. Shetland potatoes and coleslaw accompanied the superstar of the meal. Totally appropriate for Laird's first night in his new home and for Sue's last night this trip to Shetland.

After we got done eating we took our wine out and stood and watched the beacon make its lonely revolutions in the sky.

The Keeper and Crew,
Sharma

Date sent: Saturday, 11 September 1999
Subject: **Exploring the Cliffs and the North**
To: @LIST5E23.PML

Greetings,

Susie left on the 7:10 am bus to begin the long trip back to Florida. It is still hard to believe that a bus comes and picks us up at the lighthouse's front gate. The big decision of the day was where we would walk, as it is a bright and clear day. Since I am the resident expert I chose a walk I had never done before. I know it doesn't make any sense but it is one I was afraid to do alone. We are going to try to walk north to the end of the Eshaness peninsula if we can. It looks like a long way on the map. We would be following the coastline that overlooks the Eshaness Cliffs.

The first big challenge is walking around Calder's Geo. Calder's Geo, located just north of the car-park, is a steep crevice where the sea has chiseled into cliffs. It has an underground spring or river flowing out toward the sea. If the geo wasn't there you could reach the cliffs by Moo Stack in a matter of minutes. Moo Stack is world famous and may be one of the most photographed pieces of rock in Shetland. According to the *Dictionary of Scottish Place Names* by Mike Darton the name comes from 'Mool [Shetland] meaning Headland'. Letters often get dropped in place names so I figured it meant a stack off a promontory or cliff. That must be the answer because it certainly does not look anything like a cow.

Nothing is easily accessible in the Shetlands and so it took us about fifteen minutes to reach the area that overlooks Moo Stack. It is not flat walk but up and down hills and around lochs. Dean is driving me crazy. He seems to have no fear of the cliffs' edges and is constantly scaring me standing right on the rim. Marylou is almost as adventurous as Dean. I find myself constantly screaming at them not to get too close to the edge. Finally I decided the best thing for me to do was to ignore them as I would give myself a heart attack if I kept watching.

The hike was worth all the worry and effort involved. I had seen a picture taken by Colin Baxter of our lighthouse in the distance with the cliffs and sea stacks in the foreground. His picture is stunning but not nearly as striking as the real thing. Looking south, the sea stacks and the rugged cliffs are in the foreground and in the far distance a wee lighthouse sits at the top of its cliff overseeing all. I have been told many times that the lighthouse is on the highest point along the shoreline on this side of the island. The view from the north end of the cliffs proves it beyond a shadow of a doubt. Dean is fascinated with all of the sea caves at the bottom of the cliffs. Thank goodness the area is craggy and slippery or he would be down there with his head in the caves.

For the first time on any of my jaunts we met two other hikers. They were heading north up the cliff line and told us that the waterfall at the Holes of Scraada was exploding with water and cascading beautifully. Dean wanted to see the broch located on the island in the Loch of Houlland and the falls was just below the loch so we turned away from the cliffs. By the way, this is the same broch that took me two trips to get brave enough to visit in May.

In May I completely missed the waterfall or maybe it did not have any water at that time of year. The music of the water hitting the rocks was lyrical. It was so charming to me that I took four or five pictures of it. No one else was as fascinated with it as I was. Maybe that is another thing that makes the area around our lighthouse home so popular. There is something for everyone.

Dean was interested in exploring the broch. Houlland Broch walls are tumbling down yet in some areas the wall reaches thirteen feet above the water. What is unique is it is such a small island. I wonder if the ancient people built the island or if the island was there and they just used it. My imagination is constantly working over time trying to figure out the why and where for all of the prehistoric stuff. I keep hoping I will find a prehistoric artefact, just like I keep hoping I will see a pod of Orcas. You don't have to write back and tell me. I know I never seem to be satisfied.

The Explorer,
Me

Date sent: Sunday, 12 September 1999
Subject: **Tourists**
To: @LIST5E23.PML

Greetings All,

It is a quiet Sunday at Eshaness, or at least inside the lighthouse.
All of us have been outside doing various homey type things
such as washing clothes. Once again we forgot to do it at night
to take advantage of the lower electricity rates. Since our rates at
home are always the same no matter what time of day it is, that
lesson has yet to be learned. Ray has taken over my office for his
painting. It has satisfactory light and allows him to spread out
his artist supplies as the only furniture in that room is my corner
desk and a futon chair.

The office window is on the west side of the lighthouse
facing the sea. The clothesline lies between the window and the
sea. When Ray left his painting to join us for a cup of tea today
he announced the washing was horizontal. A little concerned
that our clothes were on their way to Iceland I went to check.
They were clearly flying horizontal with the ground but those
good old storm pegs were holding tight.

One of the things I have liked most about Scotland is that in
many areas Sunday as a day of rest still exists. In the United
States, Sunday is like any other day with all of the stores open,
people working at their regular job, doing something round the
house, or shopping. In all of the Scottish homes in which we
have spent significant time Sunday is a day when you do only
the necessary things, take a nap, or spend time with family. I like
that and am determined the lighthouse will observe Sunday as a
day of rest. We are sort of forced into it since there is no bus
service. But, there is a problem spelled: T-O-U-R-I-S-T. Sunday is
the major day for tourists at Eshaness. First, there is a tour bus
that arrives around morning teatime. This huge bus pulls up and
masses of people emerge with camera in hand. First the lines of
tourists go around the bus to take pictures of the cliffs, which

takes all of five minutes. Then they come back and take a picture of the lighthouse. The best thing for the inhabitants of the lighthouse to do is to hide. If you are in the yard, the tourists watch you until they think you are not busy or close enough to the fence so they can wander over to talk to you. That is fine I suppose but we did not come out here to talk to tourists especially on a peaceful Sunday. I know the beauty here belongs to all but the nicest times are when no one else is around and it is all ours.

Most of the tourists respect the sign on the fence that says 'Private House Stay Out', but there have been exceptions. One day I found two couples inside the fence and they were trying to move the sundial. The bronze sundial was custom made for Eshaness and is an important part of the history of the lighthouse. When the lighthouses were first built the sundials were used to time the lights. The Northern Lighthouse Board removed all the dials when they removed the keepers, leaving only the granite columns. The couple that owned Eshaness before us had gotten permission from the Northern Lighthouse Board to have a bronze replacement made and put on the column. The blade is shaped specifically for this location and keeps excellent time. The tourists were physically trying to move it. You can't imagine how fast I was at getting out there to tell them to get on the other side of the fence. This must have been a problem for the former owners also as they had placed barbed wire on the fence by the sundial so no one could reach over and touch it.

It is not uncommon to see tourists on the west side of the lighthouse since the blowhole is of great interest to many of them. Technically they are not on our land when they climb down to the blowhole but it is annoying to see them out the bedroom windows.

Only once have tourists come up and looked in the window and that was in May when I was alone. It frightened me a lot. For the next two nights I shut the shutters so no one could peek in the windows. Shutting the shutters is not popular with me because I like to watch the beacon as it moves from window to window. It is a constant reminder that it is a lighthouse.

The most common question we get asked by tourists is 'Is there a toilet in the lighthouse we can use?' The answer of course is no but they still ask. There is no doubt in my mind if we wanted to establish a small tearoom at the lighthouse it would be hugely successful. Dean and I are both committed to not doing anything like that. Granted the lighthouse is a historical building, I do have not a problem with people taking pictures of it as long as they leave us alone. First and foremost it is our home and for that reason I am anti-tourist, especially when they come and ruin my Sunday.

Grumpy Keeper,
Sharma

Date sent: Monday, 13 September 1999
Subject: **Excursion**
To: @LIST5E23.PML

Hi! All!

Food was running low. A list of household items which we could not live without had developed again. We seemed to be getting along just fine but we were always adding more 'necessities' to the list. Raymond had painted a beautiful watercolor I wanted to get framed. He had film he wanted developed that could mean more paintings for me. So we called Bertie last night to pick us up at 9:50 am so we could make a trip to Lerwick by bus. When we got up we weren't sure we should go to town, as it was rainy and not very nice. Checking the computer all the weather sites said it was going to clear so we braved the elements and off to Lerwick we went.

As always we met some interesting people on the bus. The bus is one place where we Americans get lessons in pronunciation. The locals help us sort out some mistakes we are making in our speech as well as giving us the latest gossip. This trip we found out that the part of the road where the Atlantic Ocean comes up to the road's edge on the south side and the North Sea does the same on the north side is not called Mavis Grind (as in 'chop up') but Mavis Grind ('grind' like grin). It is hard for Americans to get used to the local pronunciation of names. The airport is not Sumburgh (like Edinburgh) but 'Sumbru' (as in *bru*nch.) The locals call the place we live 'Eshness'. The 'a' just disappears. Another even stranger thing is that Eshaness is spelled two ways – Eshaness or Esha Ness. I have no idea which is correct but it might be worth investigating. Many of the terms here are Norwegian in origin so it's difficult for us to figure out.

By the time we arrived in Lerwick the sun was out and it was becoming a beautiful day. Usually when I take the bus to Lerwick I go for a cup of tea and then shop before lunch. Dean would have no part of that. It just so happens that the bus station is right in front of an Indian restaurant. It took about two seconds to decide that is where we were having lunch. Here I thought we would go to a place that specialized in Shetland food and instead we were eating Indian food in Shetland.

After an excellent meal we went about our shopping which included dropping the film off to be developed and going to the wine shop. You can tell what our priorities were. While we waited for the film to be developed we took the picture to be framed and shopped for those essential household items we could not live without. Once in a while it is difficult living 'at the end of the distribution chain' as Dean calls it. We were not able to get most of the items so I guess they will not be essential.

Next stop was the library. It is a pleasant place to rest your feet and stay toasty warm when you are spending most of the day in the town. We felt like we had found a rare jewel when we found a book on how to cook with and run the Rayburn. Dean was convinced we were at the end of our problems with the stove. I sure hope he is right.

After picking up the film we went to the Toll Clock for tea and biscuits where we looked at the photographs. We were excited because there were some really great shots and would mean more original watercolors from our artist in residence.

Strengthened by tea and scones we were ready to tackle the Co-op for groceries. I was becoming familiar with the store but am still thrown by things like ten or fifteen different kinds of potatoes. I definitely need an instructor on what potatoes to buy. Tom failed me here as he raises his own 'tatties' and is therefore not an expert on what the store has. After much frustration and a great deal of help from other shoppers we had most of the items on the list. One American way of doing things that might have been of help in the grocery area was larger containers. In the US our containers are much larger than those available in the UK. If I could get those big containers I would not have to make so many trips to town. But, as I learned this trip, a half-gallon of milk would not fit in my brand new refrigerator. So it may not be a container problem but an appliance issue.

After grocery shopping we got a taxi and went back to the bus station and loaded everything on the bus. Once again I was embarrassed about how much of the luggage area we took up. I was sure some of the people on that bus were feeding more people than we were but they did not have so many bags.

Tired Shopper

Date sent: Tuesday, 14 September 1999
Subject: **Glorious Blue Day**
To: @LIST5E23.PML

Greetings and Salutations,

The sun is shining. The sky is a light blue with not one cloud. The ocean along with the lochs have turned bright periwinkle blue. The waves are sparkling white and the fields are a bright yellow green. It is a colorful day. Shetland is a place that is always changing colors but I have to admit I really like the glorious blue of today.

We have some wind. Does that surprise anyone? It is warm. Dean has all the doors open to air out the house, which will also let in flies. We have the most gigantic houseflies here. They are the most robust flies I have ever seen. Tom said one day he came in and the floor was covered with huge deceased flies. Not a pleasant thought if you ask me. I am trying to get Dean not to let any of those big critters in the house

For lunch we had sandwiches and crisps down on the rocks where we could watch the fishing boats. It seems like every fisherman in Shetland is out today or at least out on the west side.

I took a picture of the lighthouse reflected in one of the lochans behind the car-park. If the photo captured the way it actually looked I should be able to enter the Lighthouse Board's Calendar competition. Eshaness does provide magnificent photo opportunities. Ray is going to do two watercolor paintings from the photos we had developed yesterday. I am taking most of the paintings home to be framed and hung there. Tom has picked out a photograph he really likes and Ray will probably do that for him.

Wood for starting the Rayburn is getting low. Marylou, Dean and I are off to gather driftwood. We found a geo down by Stenness that had lots of driftwood. It is a quite a hike down there and back. Maybe it is just another excuse to be outside but if it gets cold the wood will help get that monster Rayburn going.

You'll know it was a magnificent day when I tell you that all four of us went out to hang up clothes this morning. The clothesline being on the sea side provides such good views you find yourself getting sidetracked from the business of drying clothes.

The Group Hanging Out at the Lighthouse

Date sent: Wednesday, 15 September 1999
Subject: **Seals and Otters**
To: @LIST5E23.PML

Greeting and Salutations,

We are washing sheets and towels so we can all go out and hang up clothes again. Actually we are doing it because the weather is going to change to rain and gales for the weekend. For those of you who thinking hanging clothes on the line is a pain in comparison with sticking them in a dryer, you haven't hung clothes out surrounded by the ocean. Definitely hanging clothes has become one of the favorite activities here. Not only does the sea surround you but also you feel the wind in your face and can smell the ocean while you do something useful. The wind can be a problem. Sometimes it will come along and grab the garments right out of your hands. Then you have to move fast to get them before they go over the cliff into the sea. We haven't lost anything yet. Or the wind is so strong it wraps the clothes around the line and they get tangled. I can see them out of the office window and the clothes are still attached to the clothesline blowing straight toward the sea. Every day I become a bigger and bigger fan of storm pegs. I do not understand how these tiny yellow gadgets work but we never loose anything.

Our big item for the day was going to the seal rocks and sitting on the rock ledges to watch the seals sun themselves and do whatever it is they do in the water. We cannot figure out whether they are just swimming or fishing but they come up every few minutes for air. They are fat so we have decided seals on this coast are well supplied with food. They seem to be naturally curious about our activities as they often come out of the water and seem to stare at us. I do not know if they have good enough eyesight to actually see but it certainly looks like they do. Probably they are thinking, 'What are those strange fish doing up there on the land?'

The big excitement of the day is that Ray saw a sea otter; the first we have spotted near Eshaness. The otter was fishing and dragging his catch up on the beach. Tom saw one yesterday when he went to Stenness beach to check his lobster creels. The one he saw ran from near the croft house directly past him and into the water. I am fuming because I have not seen one. My number one activity tomorrow is to go down to the seal rocks and sit and watch for them. I might even go it if is raining, depending on how much rain.

Dean is up on the roof filming with the video camera and fixing something. It is great on the roof with the views in all directions.

The fish van supplied us with haddock and salmon yesterday. We had haddock last night and plan to have salmon tonight. Last night I tried an old Shetland recipe where you batter the fish fillets with oatmeal and broil them. It was remarkably tasty. We are having the salmon broiled and dressed with lime sauce tonight. We may be remote but the food at this hotel is first class.

Tom is coming over for tea and a blether this afternoon. Actually the big draw is a pineapple upside down cake I baked this morning. Isn't it terrible when your whole day is scheduled around afternoon tea? Great life and Dean says this is the way it should be.

The Cook,
Sharma

Date sent: Thursday, 16 September 1999
Subject: **Otter Alert!**
To: @LIST5E23.PML

Greetings,

We went down to the seal rocks to see if we could see the otter. Dean was climbing around on the rocks at sea level. Rock climbing seems to be Dean's obsession. I have finally leaned not to watch as he scares me to death. It just makes him angry if I shout at him, which probably endangers him more by distracting him. While he was climbing around an otter strolled up within a few feet of him. The otter became interested in Dean and started to follow him. We were all afraid the otter would bite Dean but he kicked at it and it scurried away. I suppose he thought Dean was something good to eat or maybe he was just curious. He scurried all over the rocks and even Ray, Marylou and I got an excellent look at him.

I had never been that close to a sea otter. He was bigger than the river otters I had seen but resembled in some ways a drowned rat. He had a long tail and a pointed nose. While Dean was down on the rocks he met a seal that was exceptionally curious about us. He spent a few minutes studying Dean. He must have found Dean rather humdrum as he quickly went back to whatever it is they do when they are under water.

It is warm here but the mist is pretty heavy so it is what I would call a gray day. When I am back in the States I call this type of day a 'Scotland Day'. They are peaceful and quiet as the fog subdues everything.

I have known since we bought Eshaness that it sits two hundred feet in the air on a cliff. As I have mentioned in previous e-mails, you can get a good sense of the lighthouse's elevation when you walk north along the cliffs. Today we found a place much closer where you can actually see the bottom of the two hundred foot cliff that the lighthouse sits on. After seeing that I will never venture very close to the edge of the rocks behind the lighthouse. From the edge it is an abrupt drop straight down to the sea.

We are going into Lerwick tomorrow to see an accountant. Since one of my publishers is located in the United Kingdom and pays me in Pound Sterling we have to find out more details about the double taxation arrangement between the US and UK. Dean will also inspect the BBC Shetland studio. He would like to start broadcasting from Shetland next trip. Being a new studio it should be more than adequate to make the hook up with WJR back in Detroit. The software that allows him to answer questions can be put on a laptop so it will almost be like broadcasting from home.

Morning tea is about ready so I had better go. Tom brought us his favorite buns from a bakery in town so I am looking forward to tasting them.

We are getting into a pleasant habit of having tea with Tom every afternoon. We found a recipe for Tom's Chocolate Gâteau so Marylou and I baked it for him today. It is a chocolate cake with raspberry jam and whipped cream in between chocolate layers and more whipped cream on top of the cake. It sounds wonderful.

Sharma

Date sent: Saturday, 18 September 1999
Subject: **Star Light Star Bright**
To: @LIST5E23.PML

Hi!

Yesterday was the first time I did not get my daily note written to you this trip. I was thrilled that a couple of you missed it. We were in Lerwick for most of the day seeing solicitors and accountants trying to get our business arrangements set up here. Then we rented a car and stopped at some of the places we pass by on the bus. Last night we went to the St Magnus Hotel for dinner. The St Magnus is where we stayed when we looked at Eshaness last January. Dean loved the food. Tom and I had gone back in May for tea but this was our first trip for dinner since January. The St Magnus is a listed building made of Norwegian pine that was brought over by ship. We wanted Ray and Marylou to see the inside. Once again everyone ate the local catch. I guess all of us are happy with Shetland's fish.

Driving back was the first time I had seen the lighthouse from any distance at night. You start seeing it as a dot of light about five miles away. Then for a while it is just a beam of light showing behind the dark hills. When you finally reach the top of the head it sits on it you can see the light revolving from the tower in the darkness. It was a crystal clear night. A beautiful half moon was reflected in all of the voes surrounding the road. It was light enough to see Dore Holm cast a shadow on the ocean surface. When we parked the car at the lighthouse it was amazing how you could see all the bright stars. Every once in a while the gray ghost of the beacon would zip by and make them a little dimmer. It was one of those special moments.

Today we are going to the Northern Isles of Yell and Unst to see the bird preserve and Muckle Flugga Lighthouse, so I may not write a long note until tomorrow morning – as it is such a beautiful sunny day we want to take advantage of it.

Star Bright Dazzled,
The Lighthouse Keeper

Date sent: Sunday, 19 September 1999
Subject: **The Northern Isles**
To: @LIST5E23.PML

Greetings on a Quiet Sunday,

We have safely returned from our trip yesterday to the Northern Isles, Yell and Unst. As you head north you pass very close to Sullom Voe, the huge oil terminal. It could have turned out to be quite ugly but it has been painted to blend in with the surrounding hills so it not as bad as I thought it would be. The first part of our adventure was to catch the 'Roll on – Roll off' ferry at Toft that takes you to Yell. This was a twenty-minute ferry ride and no real bother. We did not see too much of Yell as our ultimate destination was Unst. We stopped and had tea and scones at Gutcher before we took the ferry to Unst. After we had tea we went to get into the ferry queue but there was no queue. We discovered the ferries have a different schedule on Saturday so we decided to see if we could find the Gaada Stack, which is on the front of Colin Baxter's Shetland book. We never found it because, as I discovered later, the stack is on Foula not Yell. I wonder if I will ever get these islands straight. We did see the White Lady of Yell, which is a magnificent statue that honors deceased fisherman.

Finally we were able to make the ten-minute ride to Unst. I visited Unst last May with Charles Tait. We took pictures of the castle and drove up to Hermaness Bird Reserve. We did not try the mountain road to see Muckle Flugga as it is pretty treacherous and Marylou was not keen on driving it.

The best part of our visit to Unst was the great haddock I had at the Balta Sound Hotel. Dean loved the boat museum so it was a successful day for all.

We got up this morning to clouds but we walked down to the seal rocks anyway. This is Dean's last day so we did not want to waste the opportunity and the sun had broken through by the time we got there. Many seals were playing in the water but Dean's otter had disappeared.

Ray, Marylou and I are using the car to run around the neighborhood to see the sights. There are many crofts nestled in the hills within a five-mile radius of the lighthouse road. We even stumbled upon Tom's house and met his dogs. A stonewall and roses of all colors surrounded his two-hundred-year-old croft house. He said it only took him ten years to get the roses started. All the time we were talking about my wanting to grow roses he never told me he had beautiful ones.

Ray stopped and took lots of photos that hopefully will turn into gorgeous paintings. He finished a superb painting of the lighthouse with its reflection in the lochan in front of the gate. I am taking it home to hang over our fireplace on the farm.

I did the washing and hung it out but brought it back in within thirty minutes because I thought it was going to rain.

Low and behold the sun is out again. This ocean-front living is a challenge with the different weather patterns, or maybe it is better to say without weather patterns. It is warm with the temperature probably in the seventies but there is a stiff south-easterly wind.

Dean is finishing up his little repair jobs. He feels a strong commitment to maintaining the lighthouse to the standards that the keepers did. He even spent time polishing the brass. I asked him after his ten days here how he liked it and his answer is 'Why do I have to go home?' I think his favorite activity is climbing the rocks and being down by the sea. Eating seafood is running a close second.

After supper Dean and I went out and stood arm in arm on the hill behind the lighthouse and watched the light go around. It was a glorious moment but also sad since he was going to have to leave.

Leaving Eshaness is the hardest part of being at Eshaness. It is a different world. You know the contrast with the world back home will haunt you.

Me

Date sent: Monday, 20 September 1999
Subject: **Rainy Day**
To: @LIST5E23.PML

Greetings,

The rain is just hammering on the windows. I am doing a wash and hanging it on a clothesline we have strung from the top of the doors so that the clothes can hang above the Rayburn.
With all the company I have fallen a little behind on the Scottish Radiance correspondence so I am catching up on my e-mail.
Dean left yesterday and I miss him already. There is no one to go out into the rain and get coal for the Rayburn. Just kidding!

I do miss him though. He had a first-rate time scrambling

around on the rocks. He scared me to death many times because he went places I would never dare. I wish I were brave or foolish enough, whichever is correct, to do things like that. Then I would have been nose to nose with the otter. He was pleased with the BBC studio here and he can broadcast in the future if they can get all the technical things figured out. That will be a huge advantage, as it will allow him not to have to rush back to the US so quickly.

Tom and I went into town yesterday to run a few errands. I couldn't believe it when we went down to a big Russian fishing trawler where Tom knew someone. They gave us a big bucket full of herring free. Tom is going to clean them and we are going to try having them for dinner. I have never had fresh herring so it will be an interesting trial.

Going into my last week for this stay I love Eshaness even more than I did before. It is so charming, peaceful and yet can be violent and exciting. Everyone must get tired of my saying how beautiful it is but the bottom line is, it is stunning. One of the advantages is that there are no people except the tourists and they hardly ever show up on a rainy day. Surprisingly they do show up on extremely stormy days to take pictures of the high surf.

Ray has done some marvelous paintings. He is working on one of the cliffs this morning. This one is destined to be a gift to Tom for all of his help this trip. We have decided that the cliffs are what everyone knows so Tom should have a picture of them.

Dean took home the picture of the lighthouse in the early morning reflected in the lochans.

Today is fish van day so we hope to buy a different type of fish this morning.

Well, on to stacked up e-mail.

Catching Up,
Sharma

Date sent: Wednesday, 22 September 1999
Subject: **Daffodils, Roses and Heather**
To: @LIST5E23.PML

Greetings,

I have been out planting daffodil bulbs. It is a beautiful sunny, warm day here (70° F) so a great day to work in the garden. Tom is going to bring over some established roses from his garden and we are going to plant them this afternoon. We have an area behind the garage which might be sheltered enough to give them a chance to grow.

As soon as I've eaten lunch I am hiking into the hills to find baby heather to transplant into my little flower garden. We know the heather and the daffodils will grow but the roses are 'iffy'.

Ray and Marylou are out seeing the sights. I stayed home because I was not sure the weather would give me another day to do my flowers.

It is half day on the island. For those who do not know, that means that many stores are closed and services are not available in the afternoon. It is sort of a mini holiday for the locals and we have a whole car-park full of tourists as everyone is out taking advantage of the nice weather.

Even the midges are hanging out on the north side of the water tank. If you have not met any midges, they are tiny mosquito-like pests whose bite both itches and stings. Up to this point, midges have not bothered us to any great extent.

Lighthouse Gardener,
Sharma

Date sent: Friday, 24 September 1999
Subject: **Purpose**
To: @LIST5E23.PML

Hello!

I missed another day sending these notes but I was busy yesterday doing domestic things in preparation for leaving.

Ray and Marylou have decided to leave a day early because they are afraid fog will keep them from reaching Sumburgh early in the morning on Sunday. They are headed to Cornwall after leaving here.

Yesterday I was talking to the head engineer at Sullom Voe, Shetland's large oil terminal, and asked him the question that has always bothered me. Why do the ships still want to pay the toll to keep the lighthouses operating when they have such modern communication systems? He said communications can fail but the lights are totally reliable. However, some captains are concerned the lights are not as reliable as they used to be because the keepers are no longer monitoring the lights. Last night it was so foggy you could barely see the sundial out of the window. I thought about any ships which might be out there and was glad to see the beacon pass the window every thirteen seconds. I even went outside to see how far it penetrated into the fog. The regular range of Eshaness is twenty five miles but last night it was a lot shorter.

I am beginning to think about going home which is sad. It is too bad our beautiful farm and the lighthouse aren't closer together. I am due back in the spring and Dean is coming with me for part of the trip so it will be doubly fun.

My *Scotland – A Complete Guidebook and Road Atlas* just came off the press and I should get the first copy today in the post. I am exciting about setting up book signings for next spring. *Moonbeam Cow* will also be out within the month and that should keep me busy selling two books.

Got to go; the power is out today for some corrections so I want to bake Tom a cake for our last tea with Ray, Marylou and Tom. Ray's picture for Tom turned out extraordinary. Tom is bursting with pride that he has an original watercolor done just for him.

The Keeper

Date sent: Friday, 24 September 1999
Subject: **Stupid Sheep**
To: mistysteak@world.net

Dean,

The sheep got in the yard again and broke some of the fence. I have called the council planning board about whether the fence is protected under our historic listing. If it is not, what kind of fence do you feel we should put in? I am going to look for a temporary solution at Brae to protect the roses Tom brought over and planted. I will check the prices on new fencing for him to put in if we can get the variance. I knew we would find living in a listed building restrictive but never thought about how it might affect my gardening.

The new fence can probably wait until next spring so you could help Tom do it. Tom says the sheep are not in the fields near the lighthouse in the winter, so all is safe for that time period.

The Reluctant Shepherd,
Sharma

Date sent: Saturday, 25 September 1999
Subject: **Only One More Day**
To: @LIST5E23.PML

Hi!

Last of the company has left. Ray and Marylou departed before dinner as it is foggy here and they were driving all the way to the airport. The airport is approximately an hour and a half from here. The problem is the sheep are difficult to see on the roads in the fog and they have a tendency to sleep on the road, probably because it is warm.

The battle with the sheep continues in the front yard. Yesterday they got through the fence and were browsing around the new roses Tom planted. My call to the council planning board did not get me much information. They had to check to see if the fence is included in the listing of the house as a historical building. I will probably not find out until I get home. We did go to Brae and got some chicken wire to put around each bush. Tom has built a wood and chicken wire shelter for each rose. It will keep the sheep away and protect them somewhat from the wind. They are definitely sheep proof but whether they are weatherproof is yet to be seen. One of the tiny roses I planted last spring has two new sprouts on it so maybe we will get roses yet at Eshaness. Hurrah! Hurrah!

Last night Ray and Marylou wanted to go out for dinner so we went to Busta House in Brae. It is a beautiful huge laird's house with an abundant walled garden and pretty good size trees for Shetland. The meal was expensive but it was elegantly presented and tasted wonderful. Since I am a Bailey's Irish Cream lover I particularly like the Bailey's and chocolate chip homemade ice cream. My main course was lamb in a rosemary sauce and it was scrumptious.

The first copy of my *Scotland – A Complete Guide and Road Atlas* arrived in the post today. This one was the Globe Pequot edition and there is still to come an Appletree Press edition. It is a beautiful book and the pictures outshine my words. It is a winner as far as I can see for a guidebook. It probably will not be on sale to the general public until the first of the year.

I have to defrost the freezer as there is nothing more in it. I have a shepherd's pie cooking in the Rayburn. I think I will curl up with another Christopher Brookmyre book tonight. He is an ingenious writer with a great sense of humor.

One blessing is that Tom said he would close the shutters after I leave so I do not have to sit in the lighthouse like a prisoner on my last night like I did last spring.

The Eshaness Keeper

Date sent: Sunday, 26 September 1999
Subject: **How I Will Miss You Eshaness So Far Across the Sea**
To: @LIST5E23.PML

Greetings,

Being Sunday there were already tourists in the car-park at 10:30. Shetland has blessed me with a sunny last day with big fluffy white clouds. I am about to take a long walk and get some last pictures. It is cooler (60° F) but the fog is gone at least for a while.

A friend once said Eshaness was spiritual. Eshaness is not spiritual but so real it takes your breath away. Before Ray and Marylou left yesterday we went to the seal rocks and sat watching the birds flying around the cliffs. It is an amazing site with the white of the seagulls and the watched terns outlined on the black background of the cliffs. This trip I have became intrigued with the 'watched terns', which are migrating through right now. They are large birds the size of seagulls with black and white wings and yellow heads. Soaring above the ocean they keep looking for fish and then all of sudden they dive into the sea and come up with their lunch.

My last meal here will be a pasta salad made with fresh pollock that Tom caught today. It is a light gray fish and very tasty. The ones he brought were small and taste a great deal like tuna white meat. I boiled them in salt water and then easily picked off the flesh.

I had a major emergency this morning when a baby lamb got caught in the lighthouse's fence. Tom and I repaired the fence yesterday so it was sturdier than it had been. This poor creature got his leg and head jammed between the garage and the fence. I called Tom and he suggested I cut the fence and let the lamb free. After much pulling and shoving I was able to set him free so he could go join his mother who was calling and calling for him. I was delighted he was not hurt and I did not have to cut the fence.

I could not help but think of Moira's words as I start to close up the lighthouse until next year. I haven't even left and I miss it already.

All the positive feedback from everyone on my e-mails from Shetland is deeply appreciated. I look forward to attempting to turn them into a book as special as this place.

In order to say goodbye to the seals I walked down to the Bruddans. As always the seals were curious about this human object on shore and watched me as I stared at them. Only about eight were out today as the ocean was rough.

While I was studying the seals about twenty sandpipers surrounded me. I stood motionless so they thought I was just part of the rocks and went about their business of pecking at the ground.

This afternoon I sat out on the Orca rock and watched the cliffs. The surf at the cliffs is constantly changing and the turbulent sea made it a tempestuous place. I am considering writing my next column for Scottish Radiance on 'The Race at the Cliffs'. Sitting near the cliff's edge you are continuously in danger of being run into by a seagull. The gulls seem to have a game of hang-gliding from the cliffs out to sea and then back again. I have decided it is a contest to see which sea gull can soar the longest so the story title is about the race at the cliffs. Sounds like a children's story but we will have to see how it turns out.

Off to put a block of peat in the Rayburn and enjoy my last night before the shutters are closed tomorrow. I am establishing a tradition of going out on the last night and toasting the tower. Let it 'Shine on Me' for the last time before it moves to being only a memory in my mind.

Moira is so right in her song.

How I miss you Eshaness so far across, so far across the sea.
How I love you Eshaness so far across, so far across the sea.

This will be the last entry in the journal for this trip. I still have not conquered the Rayburn but at least it is going most of the time.

Leaving here is like the ending of a fantastic movie. You don't want it to end but know you can watch it again and again in the years to come. Dean and I will be back next spring. I look forward to the roses showing new growth and my daffodils blooming when I return from so far across the sea.

Hopeful,
The Lighthouse Keeper

Some other books published by **LUATH** PRESS

ON THE TRAIL OF

On the Trail of William Wallace

David R. Ross

ISBN 0 946487 47 2 PBK £7.99

How close to reality was *Braveheart*?

Where was Wallace actually born?

What was the relationship between Wallace and Bruce?

Are there any surviving eye-witness accounts of Wallace?

How does Wallace influence the psyche of today's Scots?

On the Trail of William Wallace offers a refreshing insight into the life and heritage of the great Scots hero whose proud story is at the very heart of what it means to be Scottish. Not concentrating simply on the hard historical facts of Wallace's life, the book also takes into account the real significance of Wallace and his effect on the ordinary Scot through the ages, manifested in the many sites where his memory is marked.

In trying to piece together the jigsaw of the reality of Wallace's life, David Ross weaves a subtle flow of new information with his own observations. His engaging, thoughtful and at times amusing narrative reads with the ease of a historical novel, complete with all the intrigue, treachery and romance required to hold the attention of the casual reader and still entice the more knowledgable historian.

74 places to visit in Scotland and the north of England

One general map and 3 location maps

Stirling and Falkirk battle plans

Wallace's route through London

Chapter on Wallace connections in North America and elsewhere

Reproductions of rarely seen illustrations

On the Trail of William Wallace will be enjoyed by anyone with an interest in Scotland, from the passing tourist to the most fervent nationalist. It is an encyclopaedia-cum-guide book, literally stuffed with fascinating titbits not usually on offer in the conventional history book.

David Ross is organiser of and historical adviser to the Society of William Wallace.

'Historians seem to think all there is to be known about Wallace has already been uncovered. Mr Ross has proved that Wallace studies are in fact in their infancy.' ELSPETH KING, Director the the Stirling Smith Art Museum & Gallery, who annotated and introduced the recent Luath edition of *Blind Harry's Wallace*.

'Better the pen than the sword!'

RANDALL WALLACE, author of *Braveheart*, when asked by David Ross how it felt to be partly responsible for the freedom of a nation following the Devolution Referendum.

On the Trail of Robert Service

GW Lockhart

ISBN 0 946487 24 3 PBK £7.99

Robert Service is famed world-wide for his eye-witness verse-pictures of the Klondike goldrush. As a war poet, his work outsold Owen and Sassoon, and he went on to become the world's first million selling poet. In search of adventure and new experiences, he emigrated from Scotland to Canada in 1890 where he was caught up in the aftermath of the raging gold fever. His vivid dramatic verse bring to life the wild, larger than life characters of the gold rush Yukon, their bar-room brawls, their lust for gold, their trigger-happy gambles with life and love. 'The Shooting of Dan McGrew' is perhaps his most famous poem:

A bunch of the boys were whooping it up in the Malamute saloon;
The kid that handles the music box was hitting a ragtime tune;
Back of the bar in a solo game, sat

Dangerous Dan McGrew,
And watching his luck was his light
o'love, the lady that's known as Lou.

His storytelling powers have brought Robert Service enduring fame, particularly in North America and Scotland where he is something of a cult figure.

Starting in Scotland, *On the Trail of Robert Service* follows Service as he wanders through British Columbia, Oregon, California, Mexico, Cuba, Tahiti, Russia, Turkey and the Balkans, finally 'settling' in France.

This revised edition includes an expanded selection of illustrations of scenes from the Klondike as well as several photographs from the family of Robert Service on his travels around the world. Wallace Lockhart, an expert on Scottish traditional folk music and dance, is the author of *Highland Balls & Village Halls* and *Fiddles & Folk*. His relish for a well-told tale in popular vernacular led him to fall in love with the verse of Robert Service and write his biography.

'A fitting tribute to a remarkable man - a bank clerk who wanted to become a cowboy. It is hard to imagine a bank clerk writing such lines as:

A bunch of boys were whooping it up...
The income from his writing actually exceeded his bank salary by a factor of five and he resigned to pursue a full time writing career.'
Charles Munn, THE SCOTTISH BANKER

'Robert Service claimed he wrote for those who wouldnt be seen dead reading poetry. His was an almost unbelievably mobile life... Lockhart hangs on breathlessly, enthusiastically unearthing clues to the poet's life.'
Ruth Thomas, SCOTTISH BOOK COLLECTOR

'This enthralling biography will delight Service lovers in both the Old World and the New.' Marilyn Wright, SCOTS INDEPENDENT

On the Trail of Robert the Bruce

David R. Ross
ISBN 0 946487 52 9 PBK £7.99

On the Trail of Robert the Bruce charts the story of Scotland's hero-king from his boyhood, through his days of indecision as Scotland suffered under the English yoke, to his assumption of the crown exactly six months after the death of William Wallace. Here is the astonishing blow by blow account of how, against fearful odds, Bruce led the Scots to win their greatest ever victory. Bannockburn was not the end of the story. The war against English oppression lasted another fourteen years. Bruce lived just long enough to see his dreams of an independent Scotland come to fruition in 1328 with the signing of the Treaty of Edinburgh. The trail takes us to Bruce sites in Scotland, many of the little known and forgotten battle sites in northern England, and as far afield as the Bruce monuments in Andalusia and Jerusalem.

67 places to visit in Scotland and elsewhere.

One general map, 3 location maps and a map of Bruce-connected sites in Ireland.

Bannockburn battle plan.

Drawings and reproductions of rarely seen illustrations.

On the Trail of Robert the Bruce is not all blood and gore. It brings out the love and laughter, pain and passion of one of the great eras of Scottish history. Read it and you will understand why David Ross has never knowingly killed a spider in his life. Once again, he proves himself a master of the popular brand of hands-on history that made *On the Trail of William Wallace* so popular.

'David R. Ross is a proud patriot and unashamed romantic.'
SCOTLAND ON SUNDAY

'Robert the Bruce knew Scotland, knew every class of her people, as no man who ruled her before or since has done. It was he who asked of her a miracle - and she accomplished it.'
AGNES MUIR MACKENZIE

On the Trail of Mary Queen of Scots

J. Keith Cheetham

ISBN 0 946487 50 2 PBK £7.99

Life dealt Mary Queen of Scots love, intrigue, betrayal and tragedy in generous measure.

On the Trail of Mary Queen of Scots traces the major events in the turbulent life of the beautiful, enigmatic queen whose romantic reign and tragic destiny exerts an undimmed fascination over 400 years after her execution.

Places of interest to visit – 99 in Scotland, 35 in England and 29 in France.

One general map and 6 location maps.

Line drawings and illustrations.

Simplified family tree of the royal houses of Tudor and Stuart.

On the Trail of Mary Queen of Scots is for everyone interested in the life of perhaps the most romantic figure in Scotland's history; a thorough guide to places connected with Mary, it is also a guide to the complexities of her personal and public life.

'In my end is my beginning'
MARY QUEEN OF SCOTS

'...the woman behaves like the Whore of Babylon' JOHN KNOX

On the Trail of John Muir

Cherry Good

ISBN 0 946487 62 6
PBK UK £7.99

Follow the man who made the US go green. Confidant of presidents, father of American National Parks, trailblazer of world conservation and voted a Man of the Millennium in the US, John Muir's life and work is of continuing relevance. A man ahead of his time who saw the wilderness he loved threatened by industrialisation and determined to protect it, a crusade in which he was largely successful. His love of the wilderness began at an early age and he was filled with wanderlust all his life.

'Only by going in silence, without baggage, can on truly get into the heart of the wilderness. All other travel is mere dust and hotels and baggage and chatter.'

JOHN MUIR

Braving mosquitoes and black bears Cherry Good set herself on his trail - Dunbar, Scotland; Fountain Lake and Hickory Hill, Wisconsin; Yosemite Valley and the Sierra Nevada, California; the Grand Canyon, Arizona; Alaska; and Canada – to tell his story. John Muir was himself a prolific writer, and Good draws on his books, articles, letters and diaries to produce an account that is lively, intimate, humorous and anecdotal, and that provides refreshing new insights into the hero of world conservation.

John Muir chronology

General map plus 10 detailed maps covering the US, Canada and Scotland

Original colour photographs

Afterword advises on how to get involved

Conservation websites and addresses

Muir's importance has long been acknowledged in the US with over 200 sites of scenic beauty named after him. He was a Founder of The Sierra Club which now has over $^1/_2$ million members. Due to the movement he started some 360 million acres of wilderness are now protected. This is a book which shows Muir not simply as a hero but as a likeable, humorous and self-effacing man of extraordinary vision.

On the Trail of Robert Burns

John Cairney

ISBN 0 946487 51 0 PBK UK £7.99

Is there anything new to say about Robert Burns?

John Cairney says itís time to trash Burns the Brand and come on the trail of the real Robert Burns. He is the best of travelling companions on this convivial, entertaining journey to the heart of the Burns story.

 Internationally known as 'the face of Robert Burns', John Cairney believes that the traditional Burns tourist trail urgently needs to find a new direction. In an acting career spanning forty years he has often lived and breathed Robert Burns on stage. *On the Trail of Robert Burns* shows just how well he can get under the skin of a character. This fascinating journey around Scotland is a rediscovery of Scotland's national bard as a flesh and blood genius.

On the Trail of Robert Burns outlines five tours, mainly in Scotland. Key sites include:

Alloway – Burns' birthplace. Tam O' Shanter draws on the witch-stories about Alloway Kirk first heard by Burns in his childhood.

Mossgiel – between 1784 and 1786 in a phenomenal burst of creativity Burns wrote some of his most memorable poems including Holy Willie's Prayer and To a Mouse.

Kilmarnock - the famous Kilmarnock edition of *Poems Chiefly in the Scottish Dialect* published in 1786.

Edinburgh - fame and Clarinda (among others) embraced him.

Dumfries - Burns died at the age of 37. The trail ends at the Burns mausoleum in St Michael's churchyard.

'For me an aim I never fash
I rhyme for fun' ROBERT BURNS

'My love affair on stage with Burns started in London in 1959. It was consumated on stage at the Traverse Theatre in Edinburgh in 1965 and has continued happily ever since' JOHN CAIRNEY

'The trail is expertly, touchingly and amusingly followed' THE HERALD

On the Trail of Bonnie Prince Charlie

David R. Ross
ISBN 0 946487 68 5 PBK £7.99
On the Trail of Bonnie Prince Charlie is the story of the Young Pretender. Born in Italy, grandson of James VII, at a time when the German house of Hanover was on the throne, his father was regarded by

 many as the righful king. Bonnie Prince Charlie's campaign to retake the throne in his father's name changed the fate of Scotland. The Jacobite movement was responsible for the '45 Uprising, one of the most decisive times in Scottish history. The suffering following the battle of Culloden in 1746 still evokes emotion. Charles' own journey immediately after Culloden is well known: hiding in the heather, escaping to Skye with Flora MacDonald. Little known of is his return to London in 1750 incognito, where he converted to Protestantism (he re-converted to Catholicism before he died and is buried in the Vatican). He was often unwelcome in Europe after the failure of the uprising and came to hate any mention of Scotland and his lost chance.

79 places to visit in Scotland and England
One general map and 4 location maps
Prestonpans, Clifton, Falkirk and Culloden battle plans
Simplified family tree
Rarely seen illustrations

Yet again popular historian David R. Ross brings his own style to one of Scotland's most famous figures. Bonnie Prince Charlie is part of the folklore of Scotland. He brings forth feelings of antagonism from some and romanticism from others, but all agree on his legal right to the throne.

Knowing the story behind the place can bring the landscape to life. Take this book with you on your travels and follow the route taken by Charles' forces on their doomed march.

'Ross writes with an immediacy, a dynamism, that makes his subjects come alive on the page.' DUNDEE COURIER

HISTORY

Reportage Scotland: History in the Making

Louise Yeoman
Foreword by Professor David Stevenson
ISBN 0 946487 61 8 PBK £9.99
Events – both major and minor – as seen and recorded by Scots throughout history.

Which king was murdered in a sewer?
What was Dr Fian's love magic?
Who was the half-roasted abbot?
Which cardinal was salted and put in a barrel?
Why did Lord Kitchener's niece try to blow up Burns's cottage?

The answers can all be found in this eclectic mix covering nearly 2000 years of Scottish history. Historian Louise Yeoman's rummage through the manuscript, book and newspaper archives of the National Library of Scotland has yielded an astonishing range of material from a letter to the king of the Picts to in Mary Queen of Scots' own account of the murder of David Riccio; from the execution of William Wallace to accounts of anti-poll tax actions and the opening of the new Scottish Parliament. The book takes pieces from the original French, Latin, Gaelic and Scots and makes them accessible to the general reader, often for the first time.

The result is compelling reading for anyone interested in the history that has made Scotland what it is today.

'*Marvellously illuminating and wonderfully readable*'. Angus Calder, SCOTLAND ON SUNDAY

'*A monumental achievement in drawing together such a rich historical harvest*' Chris Holme, THE HERALD

Blind Harry's Wallace

William Hamilton of Gilbertfield
Introduced by Elspeth King
ISBN 0 946487 43 X HBK £15.00
ISBN 0 946487 33 2 PBK £8.99

The original story of the real braveheart, Sir William Wallace. Racy, blood on every

page, violently anglophobic, grossly embellished, vulgar and disgusting, clumsy and stilted, a literary failure, a great epic.

Whatever the verdict on BLIND HARRY, this is the book which has done more than any other to frame the notion of Scotland's national identity. Despite its numerous 'historical inaccuracies', it remains the principal source for what we now know about the life of Wallace.

The novel and film *Braveheart* were based on the 1722 Hamilton edition of this epic poem. Burns, Wordsworth, Byron and others were greatly influenced by this version 'wherein the old obsolete words are rendered more intelligible', which is said to be the book, next to the Bible, most commonly found in Scottish households in the eighteenth century. Burns even admits to having 'borrowed... a couplet worthy of Homer' directly from Hamilton's version of BLIND HARRY to include in '*Scots wha hae*'.

Elspeth King, in her introduction to this, the first accessible edition of BLIND HARRY in verse form since 1859, draws parallels between the situation in Scotland at the time of Wallace and that in Bosnia and Chechnya in the 1990s. Seven hundred years to the day after the Battle of Stirling Bridge, the 'Settled Will of the Scottish People' was expressed in the devolution referendum of 11 September 1997. She describes this as a landmark opportunity for mature reflection on how the nation has been shaped, and sees BLIND HARRY'S WALLACE as an essential and compelling text for this purpose.

'*A true bard of the people*'.
TOM SCOTT, THE PENGUIN BOOK OF SCOTTISH VERSE, on Blind Harry.

'*A more inventive writer than Shakespeare*'.
RANDALL WALLACE

'*The story of Wallace poured a Scottish prejudice in my veins which will boil along until the floodgates of life shut in eternal rest*'.
ROBERT BURNS

'*Hamilton's couplets are not the best poetry you will ever read, but they rattle along at a fair pace. In re-issuing this work, the publishers have re-opened the spring from which most of our conceptions of the Wallace legend come*'.
SCOTLAND ON SUNDAY

'*The return of Blind Harry's Wallace, a man who makes Mel look like a wimp*'.
THE SCOTSMAN

A Word for Scotland

Jack Campbell
with a foreword by Magnus Magnusson
ISBN 0 946487 48 0 PBK £12.99

 'A word for Scotland' was Lord Beaverbrook's hope when he founded the *Scottish Daily Express*. That word for Scotland quickly became, and was for many years, the national newspaper of Scotland.

The pages of *A Word For Scotland* exude warmth and a wry sense of humour. Jack Campbell takes us behind the scenes to meet the larger-than-life characters and ordinary people who made and recorded the stories. Here we hear the stories behind the stories that hit the headlines in this great yarn of journalism in action.

It would be true to say 'all life is here'. From the Cheapside Street fire of which cost the lives of 19 Glasgow firemen, to the theft of the Stone of Destiny, to the lurid exploits of serial killer Peter Manuel, to encounters with world boxing champions Benny Lynch and Cassius Clay - this book offers telling glimpses of the characters, events, joy and tragedy which make up Scotland's story in the 20th century.

'As a rookie reporter you were proud to work on it and proud to be part of it - it was fine newspaper right at the heartbeat of Scotland.'
RONALD NEIL, Chief Executive of BBC Production, and a reporter on the *Scottish Daily Express* (1963-68)

'This book is a fascinating reminder of Scottish journalism in its heyday. It will be read avidly by those journalists who take pride in their profession – and should be compulsory reading for those who don't.'
JACK WEBSTER, columnist on *The Herald* and *Scottish Daily Express* journalist (1960-80)

NEW SCOTLAND

Scotland - Land and Power the agenda for land reform
Andy Wightman
foreword by Lesley Riddoch
ISBN 0 946487 70 7 PBK £5.00

Old Scotland New Scotland
Jeff Fallow
ISBN 0 946487 40 5 PBK £6.99

Notes from the North incorporating a Brief History of the Scots and the English
Emma Wood
ISBN 0 946487 46 4 PBK £8.99

SOCIAL HISTORY

Shale Voices
Alistair Findlay
foreword by Tam Dalyell MP
ISBN 0 946487 63 4 PBK £10.99
ISBN 0 946487 78 2 HBK £17.99

Crofting Years
Francis Thompson
ISBN 0 946487 06 5 PBK £6.95

LUATH GUIDES TO SCOTLAND

Mull and Iona: Highways and Byways
Peter Macnab
ISBN 0 946487 58 8 PBK £4.95

SouthWest Scotland
Tom Atkinson
ISBN 0 946487 04 9 PBK £4.95

The West Highlands: The Lonely Lands
Tom Atkinson
ISBN 0 946487 56 1 PBK £4.95

The Northern Highlands: The Empty Lands
Tom Atkinson
ISBN 0 946487 55 3 PBK £4.95

The North West Highlands: Roads to the Isles
Tom Atkinson
ISBN 0 946487 54 5 PBK £4.95

TRAVEL AND LEISURE

Edinburgh's Historic Mile
Duncan Priddle
ISBN 0 946487 97 9 PBK £2.99

Edinburgh and Leith Pub Guide
Stuart McHardy
ISBN 0 946487 80 4 PBK £4.95

Pilgrims in the Rough: St Andrews beyond the 19th hole
Michael Tobert
ISBN 0 946487 74 X PBK £7.99

WALK WITH LUATH

Mountain Days & Bothy Nights
Dave Brown and Ian Mitchell
ISBN 0 946487 15 4 PBK £7.50

The Joy of Hillwalking
Ralph Storer
ISBN 0 946487 28 6 PBK £7.50

Scotland's Mountains before the Mountaineers
Ian Mitchell
ISBN 0 946487 39 1 PBK £9.99

LUATH WALKING GUIDES

Walks in the Cairngorms
Ernest Cross
ISBN 0 946487 09 X PBK £4.95

Short Walks in the Cairngorms
Ernest Cross
ISBN 0 946487 23 5 PBK £4.95

FICTION

But n Ben A-Go-Go
Matthew Fitt
ISBN 0 946487 82 0 HBK £10.99

The Bannockburn Years
William Scott
ISBN 0 946487 34 0 PBK £7.95

The Great Melnikov
Hugh MacLachlan
ISBN 0 946487 42 1 PBK £7.95

Grave Robbers
Robin Mitchell
ISBN 0 946487 72 3 PBK £7.99

NATURAL SCOTLAND

Wild Scotland: The essential guide to finding the best of natural Scotland
James McCarthy
Photography by Laurie Campbell
ISBN 0 946487 37 5 PBK £7.50

'Nothing but Heather!'
Gerry Cambridge
ISBN 0 946487 49 9 PBK £15.00

Scotland Land and People
An Inhabited Solitude
James McCarthy
ISBN 0 946487 57 X PBK £7.99

The Highland Geology Trail
John L Roberts
ISBN 0946487 36 7 PBK £4.99

Rum: Nature's Island
Magnus Magnusson
ISBN 0 946487 32 4 PBK £7.95

Red Sky at Night
John Barrington
ISBN 0 946487 60 X PBK £8.99

Listen to the Trees
Don MacCaskill
ISBN 0 946487 65 0 PBK   £9.99

FOLKLORE

The Supernatural Highlands
Francis Thompson
ISBN 0 946487 31 6 PBK £8.99

Scotland: Myth, Legend and Folklore
Stuart McHardy
ISBN: 0 946487 69 3 PBK 7.99

Tall Tales from an Island
Peter Macnab
ISBN 0 946487 07 3 PBK £8.99

Tales from the North Coast
Alan Temperley
ISBN 0 946487 18 9 PBK £8.99

BIOGRAPHY

Tobermory Teuchter: A first-hand account of life on Mull in the early years of the 20th century
Peter Macnab
ISBN 0 946487 41 3 PBK £7.99

Bare Feet and Tackety Boots
Archie Cameron
ISBN 0 946487 17 0 PBK £7.95

Come Dungeons Dark
John Taylor Caldwell
ISBN 0 946487 19 7 PBK £6.95

MUSIC AND DANCE

Highland Balls and Village Halls
GW Lockhart
ISBN 0 946487 12 X PBK £6.95

Fiddles & Folk: A celebration of the re-emergence of Scotland's musical heritage
GW Lockhart
ISBN 0 946487 38 3 PBK £7.95

SPORT

Over the Top with the Tartan Army (Active Service 1992-97)
Andrew McArthur
ISBN 0 946487 45 6 PBK £7.99

Ski & Snowboard Scotland
Hilary Parke
ISBN 0 946487 35 9 PBK £6.99

POETRY

Poems to be read aloud
Collected and with an introduction by Tom Atkinson
ISBN 0 946487 00 6 PBK £5.00

Luath Press Limited

committed to publishing well written books worth reading

LUATH PRESS takes its name from Robert Burns, whose little collie Luath (*Gael.*, swift or nimble) tripped up Jean Armour at a wedding and gave him the chance to speak to the woman who was to be his wife and the abiding love of his life. Burns called one of *The Twa Dogs* Luath after Cuchullin's hunting dog in *Ossian's Fingal*. Luath Press grew up in the heart of Burns country, and now resides a few steps up the road from Burns' first lodgings in Edinburgh's Royal Mile.

Luath offers you distinctive writing with a hint of unexpected pleasures.

Most UK and US bookshops either carry our books in stock or can order them for you. To order direct from us, please send a £sterling cheque, postal order, international money order or your credit card details (number, address of cardholder and expiry date) to us at the address below. Please add post and packing as follows: UK – £1.00 per delivery address; overseas surface mail – £2.50 per delivery address; overseas airmail – £3.50 for the first book to each delivery address, plus £1.00 for each additional book by airmail to the same address. If your order is a gift, we will happily enclose your card or message at no extra charge.

Luath Press Limited
543/2 Castlehill
The Royal Mile
Edinburgh EH1 2ND
Scotland
Telephone: 0131 225 4326 (24 hours)
Fax: 0131 225 4324
email: gavin.macdougall@luath.co.uk
Website: www.luath.co.uk